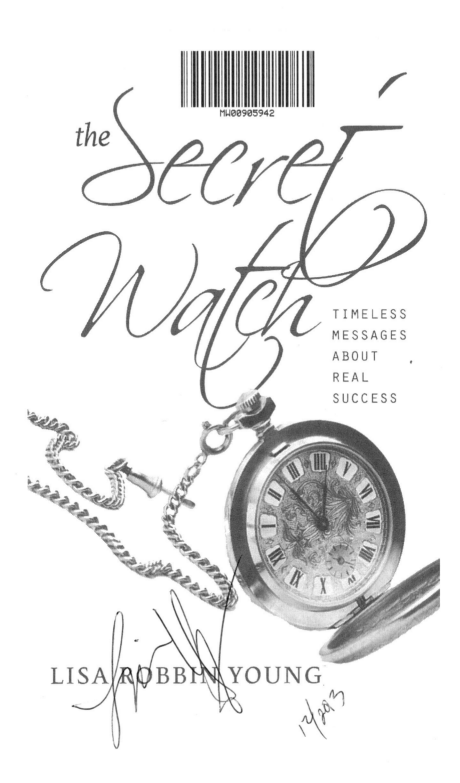

the

Secret
Watch

TIMELESS
MESSAGES
ABOUT
REAL
SUCCESS

LISA ROBBIN YOUNG

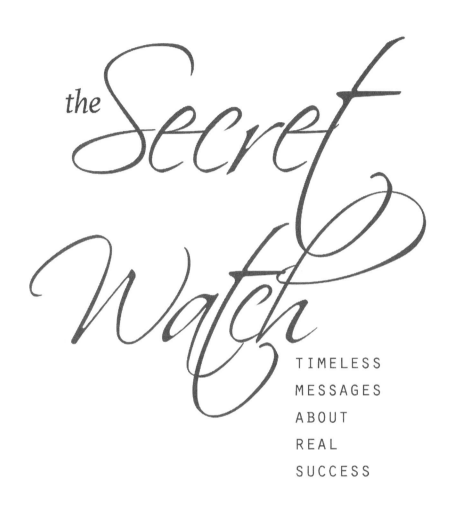

the Secret Watch

TIMELESS
MESSAGES
ABOUT
REAL
SUCCESS

LISA ROBBIN YOUNG

Edited by Andrea Patten
Cover design by Lori Paquette

ISBN: 978-1481024266

QUANTITY DISCOUNTS are available on bulk purchases of this book for educational and gift purposes, or as a premium for certain products and services, subject to publisher approval. Special books or book excerpts can also be created to fit specific needs. For information please contact Ark Entertainment Media, 835 Southwood Drive, Fenton, MI 48430 (810) 391-9648

For those who strive

to build a Noble Empire,

and live an inspired life.

Contents

Introduction

Entrepreneurs dream of success.

We want it. We chase it. Some of us write down a number -- or certain other goals -- and begin bowing at the altar of "if only."

"If only I could have x, then I'd be successful."

"If only y would happen, then I'd see some success."

Far too few of us take the time to define success for ourselves; to step in to full ownership of success and what it can really mean.

The most highly successful people I know look like founding members of the "Have It All" Club: loving family, profitable work, a calendar as full as they want it to be and plenty of people who want a piece of their action. We look at their success from the outside and believe everything works perfectly. Effortlessly. It looks as if these superstars surely have a "special something" that makes it possible for them (and not the rest of us) to have real success.

It's too bad we let ourselves off the hook like that. When I talk with members of "the club," two things are absolutely clear: first, they work incredibly hard to achieve that balance in their lives and, second, they are no more special than anyone else, except perhaps in these important ways:

> *They've given up on the traditional definition of work-life balance.*
>
> *They've defined -- and experience -- success on their own terms.*

Let's -- for at least a moment -- give up the definition of work-life balance that resembles the scales of justice. Let's substitute a more useful image: perhaps a wire walker, an acrobat or an accomplished juggler. They perform with such ease that we forget the significant investment of time, energy and training it takes to develop that level of skill. Again, an outsider's perspective.

As an entrepreneur, you know what takes place 'behind the scenes' in your own business. It can be messy -- downright ugly -- at times. But, just like the wire walker arriving at the platform on other side to thunderous applause, that investment of resources often brings a flood of blessings and increased awareness of our good fortune. In other words: we experience the results of our efforts.

True balance is more holistic than juggling or even wire walking: it's rarely 'one wrong move' that brings everything crashing down around us. In the real world, balance is based on the myriad choices we make every day, from one moment to the next. Ultimately it is those choices, compounded over time, that determine our success in business or in life.

That's the story of Tina, as told in *The Secret Watch*. As the story unfolds, Tina's eyes are opened to the inborn gifts she already has . . . her 'undeniable gifts.' She becomes empowered to re-define success on terms that make her life and her work far more rewarding for everyone involved.

I've been writing and telling stories for years. Early in my life I learned that engaging someone in a story helps make the message more memorable. The other thing I learned (thanks to Martin Jennings, my high school drama teacher) is to 'share what you know.'

Tina's story is, in some ways, my own. I've been a single mom, an entrepreneur building a business from home and a business owner with payroll to meet. I know this story well because I've lived so much of it.

So, while the story is highly personal, it also belongs to *any* entrepreneur trying to grow a dream in today's marketplace. It offers guideposts to help readers define success and reminds us -- especially parents -- that it is possible to build a "noble empire" in a way that lets your kids know what you look like.

The story begins -- both in the book and in real life -- on an airplane. Flying home from a conference, I met Stevie: a fascinating, personable, "pay it forward" kind of woman. I was journaling in the rear of the plane when she walked back from first class and 'channeled' the idea for the book. She told me, in no uncertain terms, to write a book called "The Secret Watch" because "every second tells you something special." I jotted her ideas in my journal and, when I looked up, she was gone. It was kind of spooky! By the end of the flight, I'd outlined sixty lessons for the watch.

When I finally saw her outside of baggage claim I thanked her and asked for her card. She insisted the idea was entirely meant for me to pursue and she wanted no credit at all -- another testament to her big-heartedness.

So I spent the next six months working with my friend and editor, Andrea Patten, who helped turn that outline into the story you now hold in your hands. Without her, this book would still be a mess of notes and scattered thoughts. She is a master craftswoman and I owe her a tremendous debt for her faith in this project.

The Secret Watch is a story about balance - which rarely, if ever, looks like the scales of justice. The Five Key Areas of Success can help anyone achieve a more well-rounded, fulfilled life. It is my hope that more people will embrace this definition of work-life balance and share the timeless messages of success *The Secret Watch* has for us all.

Lisa Robbin Young

Fenton, Michigan
November 1, 2012

1. Time & Attention

"The past is a ghost, the future a dream.
All we ever have is now." ~ Bill Cosby

"Howdy, folks. This is your captain," said an upbeat, confident voice from the speakers. "We're about loaded up . . . Just waitin' on one more passenger so we can close the doors and get y'all on your way to Deee-troit. Good news: it's a first class passenger, so this should be real quick. Plus, the weather's mighty fine in the Motor City. Clear and breezy. And it looks like we'll be third in line for takeoff."

"Swell," Tina said to herself, eyeing the empty seat beside her. The young businesswoman had never had a chance to fly first class before. Feeling both spoiled and discouraged, she had hoped to occupy the whole cushy row by herself. In addition, she sincerely did not want her sour outlook to infect anyone else.

"I'll just do some sketching," she thought to herself, pulling the blue journal out of her bag. "Maybe that will keep conversation to a minimum." Tina was a talented graphic artist and sketching was usually a good way for her to jump start her creative flow -- and maybe even garner a bit of privacy, too.

Moments later, a wheelchair cornered the aisle and an elderly woman stood up. She was dressed modestly, yet elegantly. Her grey wool suit barely showed its age. A small, antique pocket watch hung from a medium weight silver box chain around her neck. She shuffled around and organized herself in the seat beside Tina, waving off the assistance of the transport personnel, the gate agent, and the flight attendant.

"Oh great," grumped Tina under her breath. "Royalty." The last thing she needed was a high-maintenance seatmate who required time, energy and attention. She simply didn't have any left.

"Thank you, Dear Ones. I can manage," said the old woman, polite but firm.

"Yes ma'am, Mrs. King," the flight attendant replied, backing off a little. "Enjoy your flight."

Tina shifted uncomfortably in her seat and turned to face the window, restlessly sketching her view of the ground crew and the apron in her journal.

"First time on an airplane?" the old woman asked.

"Excuse me?" Tina asked. She wasn't paying much attention and had really hoped the old woman would leave her alone.

"Is this your first time flying, Dear One?" the old woman repeated.

"Uh, no. First time in first class, though. Probably my last, too," Tina fidgeted with her journal, irritated by her own honesty.

"Oh?" the elderly woman asked, raising an eyebrow.

Tina closed her journal and turned back toward the woman.

"I splurged on an upgrade. Normally, I fly coach, but since I don't figure I'll be flying much anymore, I cashed in all my miles to find out what life is like on the other side of the curtain," she said motioning to the partition that separates the masses from the elite few that fly in the first class cabin. There was frustration, bitterness and a bit of wistfulness in her tone.

"I see." The old woman smiled, persisting sweetly. "My name's Regina." She extended her hand to Tina who, reluctantly, grasped and shook it.

"And you are. . . ?" Regina looked at her with determination.

"I'm Tina." she said, hoping this would end the conversation. She turned back to the window. Tina really didn't like to be rude but was in absolutely no mood for conversation.

"Not much of a view from the tarmac, is there?" Regina continued, gently prodding while the captain and crew completed their pre-flight prep. The flight attendant's instructions began in the background.

"I suppose not," Tina replied. "But I'd better take it all in while I can."

She was beginning to wish she could become invisible. She did not want to take out her anger and disappointment on the old woman now seated beside her. Tina was trying to be quiet. Regina seemed nice enough, yet there was something in her demeanor and attention that kept luring Tina out of her shell, revealing more than she cared to in each little exchange. Always more comfortable sharing good news than bad, Tina tried hard to resist the compulsion to chat. She turned her attention to the evacuation instructions on the seat pocket card.

Awkwardness filled the space between the two women as each pretended to turn her full attention to crew instructions, oxygen masks, and the locations of the emergency exits.

Tina felt relieved as the flight attendants wrapped their demonstration and began final preparations for departure. In that moment she believed in her ability to re-establish both the silence and her privacy. Tina let out a soft sigh of relaxation. That sense of relief was short-lived.

"Why so gloomy, Dear One?" Regina prodded.

"She's certainly persistent," Tina said to herself as she took a deep breath. Then she remembered what her mother used to say: it's easier to make friends when you play nice. Tina put on her friendliest face and turned toward the old woman.

"I'm just a little homesick right now," Tina replied, as blankly as she could. "It's been a few days and I really miss my kids. I'd actually rather be cooking their dinner right now than sitting on this plane. Even if we *are* on the fancy side of the curtain," Tina smiled wryly. "No offense."

Tina hadn't told the entire truth. What she failed to mention was that she had taken her last bit of savings and invested it in attending a conference for start-up entrepreneurs. This trip was Tina's 'Hail Mary' effort to salvage her business. To say it had gone poorly would be optimistic. She'd made a few new friends and contacts at the conference, but that wasn't going to pay the bills.

Her husband's hours had been cut at work and the financial pinch was taking a toll on their relationship. It seemed as if the only time they ever talked anymore was when they were dealing with one money crisis or another.

Their juggling act was about to come to an end. She was fresh out of ideas to keep pace with the family's mounting debt and had hoped to sign at least one new design client during the conference. Instead, she was coming home empty-handed. She felt like a total loser. The last thing Tina wanted to do was to make small talk with an old lady on the plane, regardless of how nice she might be.

"I know just how you feel," Regina's eyes sparkled. "My son will be waiting for me at the airport. I haven't seen him in almost a year. He has been trying to get me into all that technology stuff, but you can't hug a video conferencing screen, can you?"

"Yeah. There's something about being together in person that can't be replicated, isn't there?" Tina softened. "Why has it been so long since you've seen your son?" The plane began to taxi down the runway.

Regina smiled and settled in a bit. Tina found herself considering the old woman, wondering if she, too would live into her eighties and what that might be like. "Will my business ever get off the ground, or will I be employed somewhere, picking out my gold retirement watch for years of devoted service?" she wondered as she really looked at her seatmate for the first time.

Tina suddenly realized that her attention had shifted and with it, her attitude. She was starting to see Regina in a different light.

"Between raising his own family and running my company, he has had his hands full." Regina offered her card as the plane lurched into the air and began the climb to cruising altitude. Tina immediately noticed the weight and elegance of the paper stock.

"Business consulting, huh?" Tina said. "Where were you three days ago, before this conference?" She grinned and tucked the card into the pocket of her journal.

Regina smiled. "I was making my final arrangements for . . . this flight. What happened at the conference that you'd need a business consultant?"

"It's more like what didn't happen. I wouldn't have gone at all, except I had already paid for it," Tina said grumpily. "My husband thought it would be good for me to get out of the house for a few days to refresh my outlook. Instead, I've been in knots all weekend. Everyone there was at the top of their game. Everyone except me."

Tina was surprised by how good it felt to say those words out loud.

"I see," Regina replied knowingly. "Sometimes life gets out of whack and things just start falling apart. It seems the harder you try the worse things get. I've been there myself," she said, absently stroking the watch around her neck. "More than once. There is good news. It does get better."

"Nowhere to go but up, right?" Tina laughed awkwardly.

She was interrupted by a loud 'ding' and the flight attendant's voice over the PA system.

"Ladies and gentlemen, we've reached our cruising altitude and the captain has turned off the Fasten Seat Belt sign. You are now free to move around the cabin. However we always recommend you keep your seat belt fastened whenever you are seated."

The two women looked at one another and giggled about the timing of the announcement. "Cruising altitude has a nice ring to it," Tina laughed, genuinely more relaxed than before. "I wonder when I'll get to cruising altitude in my own life."

"Indeed," Regina replied. "Tell me about your business."

Tina brightened. "Really? Well, I'm a graphic designer, but I'm not sure I can call it a business with only one client. That was the big reason for the trip. I was hoping to connect with some potential customers at the conference, and it didn't quite pan out."

Tina showed Regina a couple of sketches from her journal, including the tarmac doodle she'd been working on to avoid talking. She told Regina she had pretty much decided that coming away from this conference with no new business meant she was going to have to get a regular job.

"An entrepreneur's life might be *my* big dream, but at this stage it's just not fair to my family," she said.

"It takes courage to admit that, especially when you clearly have the talent and work ethic to run a successful company," Regina said gently.

"I don't feel particularly courageous at the moment." Tina deflected the compliment. "I feel like a loser."

"I guess it's a matter of perspective." Regina countered. "Some say the glass is half full, others say it's half empty."

Tina smiled thoughtfully. "Point taken. Thank you."

Through the remainder of the flight the two women chatted like old friends. Regina offered words of assurance and Tina scribbled notes in her journal. Tina found herself writing down quotable phrases such as "Money is a magnifier. It only amplifies what we already have." Not only was this kind old woman growing on her, she clearly knew her stuff.

As the plane touched down, their pre-flight roles reversed. It was Regina who started to bring the conversation to a close.

"Well, this is where I get off," she chuckled.

"Yeah. Me too." Tina smiled, wanting to continue their conversation. "Let me at least help you get to the gate . . . unless you want to manage that whole entourage thing again."

"Thank you, Dear One, that's very kind of you." Regina situated herself in the wheelchair as Tina collected their belongings. "Are you sure your family won't mind?"

"Nah. They won't even notice. It's much easier for my husband and the kids to wait in the cell phone lot and pick me up outside," Tina sighed.

She remembered her corporate days, when the whole family would anxiously await her return from a trip and greet her at the terminal. Invariably, she'd have a gift or two for her children from whatever far-off destination she'd visited. Her days of being met at the gate seemed like a distant memory.

"Oh." Regina seemed to be at a loss for words. "Very well then. Let's roll!"

Tina smiled and carefully wheeled Regina off the plane and up the ramp.

The young woman continued pushing the wheelchair past the gate podium and out towards baggage claim.

"Regina, I appreciate what you did for me tonight."

"What is that, Dear One?" Regina replied.

"Thank you for the time and attention you took with me. It was almost as if you were on a mission to be sure that I left my grumpy mood behind and talk with you. If you hadn't persisted, I really would have missed your words of wisdom," Tina said as the pair rolled up to the baggage carousel. "Your encouragement truly was the highlight of this trip."

LISA ROBBIN YOUNG

2. Two-Way Street

"When you cease to make a contribution, you
begin to die." -- Eleanor Roosevelt

Before Regina could respond, the two women heard
the word "Mother!" happily ring out across the
baggage claim area. A handsome man, perhaps in
his fifties, approached them. Well-groomed and
polished from head to toe, nothing seemed out of
place. Tina took special notice of his shoes. They
were so shiny they looked as if they could be made
of glass. She wondered if he was always this
immaculate or if he made a special attempt to
impress his mother.

"It's so good to see you. I trust all went well on the flight?" said the man as he bent to kiss Regina on the cheek.

"This must be your son," Tina said, stifling the urge to say something silly. She was simultaneously warmed and embarrassed to be part of their reunion.

"Yes," Regina replied. "To both of you! Tina, this is Marcus. Marcus, Tina. She has been a great help to me on the flight."

"Hardly," Tina scoffed, extending her hand to shake with Marcus. "Your mother was the best seatmate I've ever had. And assist? I'm sure you know that this little ride to the baggage carousel pales compared to the wisdom and support she shared with me on the way."

Marcus smiled as he shook Tina's hand. The grip was firm but relaxed. Powerful but not intimidating. He motioned for his driver to gather his mother's belongings. "Well, thank you for making Mother's last flight her best."

"Last flight?" Tina inquired.

"Marcus, my dear, are we ready to go?" Regina asked, ignoring Tina's question.

"Yes, Mother. Let me double-check with Robert," The look on Regina's face suggested that Marcus may have spoken out of turn: his sudden interest in helping the driver confirmed it.

"Tina," Regina said, as she stood up from the wheelchair. "I want to thank you for your company and friendship on the flight. You've been such a dear, and I appreciate you humoring this old broad tonight."

Tina smiled and was struck by the fact that the old woman seemed to be much stronger and more energetic than when she'd first sat down beside her on the flight. "As I said, it was entirely my pleasure. I never know what to expect when I get on a plane. I think if I ever get to fly again I'll make sure it's first class," she said, a bit more bravely than she felt.

"You will, Dear One, you will," Regina said, taking Tina's hands in hers. "And, before we head in separate directions, I have a little gift for you . . . to thank you for your attention and care tonight." She removed the antique pocket watch from around her neck and placed it firmly in Tina's hands. "Please take this. I want you to have it."

Tina took a step back, surprised. She opened her hand and looked down at the beautiful pocket watch. It was probably as old as Regina, maybe even older. Its shiny finish was as polished as Marcus' shoes and the case was intricately etched. It shone like it was brand new, but the styling of the fob and the ornate etching on the cover were unlike anything Tina had ever seen. This was real craftsmanship and probably an heirloom antique.

Now it was Tina's turn to fumble for the right words. "Oh, no. Thank you, but this is far too fine a gift for any small amount of effort it took to help you to the baggage claim."

Regina was insistent. "You did much, much more than escort me to baggage claim, Dear One. You were attentive to the needs of a total stranger . . . and I'm not just talking about driving the wheel chair."

"It's lovely, really it is, but I couldn't possibly. . ."

"Do you have any idea how rare it is for someone your age to allow someone my age to share my experience as a peer rather than someone's doddering old grandmother? I'm afraid you have no way of knowing how good that felt . . . at least not for a very long time."

Tina was at a loss for words but still felt uncomfortable about accepting the gift. Before she could mount another objection Marcus intervened.

"Tina, please." Marcus said as he rejoined the two women. "If Mother wants you to have it, then it's definitely meant for you."

Regina beamed at her son.

"Please, Tina? I am confident it will help you on your journey," Regina smiled. She again folded Tina's hands around the watch. This time she held them closed. The strength of the old woman's grip caught Tina by surprise.

"It may not look like much, but this little watch has been invaluable to me," Regina looked toward Marcus, who was nodding his approval. "It is a gift from both of us."

Tina smiled as she looked into the old woman's face. She had no idea how a watch could help her right now, but it was clear Regina would not take 'no' for an answer. The look on Marcus' face was equally resolute.

Tina nodded and accepted the watch. "Um, okay. Thank you."

"Whatever you do, whatever happens, promise me you won't sell it. It's very old and very precious. Like me." Regina grinned slyly at her new friend.

Tina and Marcus both chuckled. Tina promised to take care of the watch, and thanked Regina one last time as they parted company.

"Be sure to read the inscription," Marcus called over his shoulder to Tina as he walked his mother toward the chauffeur and the waiting car. "It just might surprise you."

Tina waved in acknowledgment and watched from afar as Marcus helped his mother into the limo. As the car pulled away, she pressed the button on the pocket watch. The cover sprang open and inside was an inscription, small but clear.

"Help is a two-way street. Give. Receive."

"More wisdom from my journey." Tina said, pulling out her journal, to write down the little quote.

Then she put the watch in her purse, pulled her bags from the carousel and headed for the parking lot.

It was chilly outside. A crisp breeze blew through the traffic aisle, reminding Tina that winter was fast approaching. As she sat on the bench outside the baggage claim area, Tina thought about Regina and the watch. "Why did she give it to me? I wonder if she makes a habit of giving heirlooms to strangers." Tina thought better of the situation. "Probably not, I guess. And why did her son seem equally insistent that I keep it? He doesn't know me at all. Hmm."

The inscription was certainly compelling. It seemed to capture the spirit of their conversation. Tina had gained valuable support and encouragement from a successful business owner - and a fancy silver watch to boot! She was now convinced that her imagination had not been working overtime: the conversation energized Regina, which made her seem far more powerful than the little old lady who first sat beside Tina on the plane.

She smiled at that thought before glancing once more at the the watch inscription now in her journal:

"Help is a two-way street. Give. Receive."

"Still, it just seems odd that a total stranger would give me such a valuable gift." Tina said, closing the journal cover.

Then Tina remembered the business card Regina had given her. Before she could re-open her journal to find it, a silver hatchback pulled up to the curb in front of her. The trunk popped open. It was Michael and the kids.

Tina collected her things. She lifted the lid on the cargo hatch and said hello to her family. Michael was engrossed in the sports scores on the radio. Her oldest, Natalie, was wearing headphones and listening to music; six-year-old Charlie was asleep in his booster seat. It was as if no one had heard her.

"Ahh, the irony," she thought to herself, remembering her encounter just a few moments earlier with the wealthy woman, and her equally polished son with the limo. She felt more than a little put out as she hoisted her two large suitcases into the car. Frustrated, she tried again. "How was the drive?"

No response.

"Figures," Tina thought to herself. "I've been away for nearly a week, feeling guilty about being gone and missing them like crazy. They barely know I'm here." She loaded her laptop, walked to the front of the car and climbed in.

Compared to the brisk temperature curbside, the car was warm and welcoming. "Hi, Honey," Tina said as she climbed in, trying to stay upbeat.

Her husband answered without adjusting the volume on the radio, "Hey. Ready?"

Michael was a man of few words.

Tina sighed as she buckled her seat belt, rubbed her hands together to warm her fingers, and turned to the window.

"Yep."

LISA ROBBIN YOUNG

3. Heart & Home

"I can live without money, but I cannot
live without love." -- Judy Garland

Michael pulled away from the curb and Natalie
looked up, finally realizing her mother was now
seated in the front of the car.

"Hey Mom! What'd you bring me?" she asked loudly,
speaking over the music in her headphones.

Tina tried to hide her frustration. How had things
gotten to this point? It seemed the only time her
daughter spoke to her was when she wanted
something. This sure wasn't the 'happily ever after'
she'd had in mind when she left her corporate job
to start a family. Then again, she never expected

the sudden downturn in her husband's career, either. In fact, there was so much of this life that felt like it wasn't hers, she often felt like she was sleepwalking through the life of someone else.

The last thing she wanted was to start an argument. Nor did she want to spend even one of the ninety minutes of their drive home recounting the failures of her trip. She just wanted to ride in peace. It was as if all the calming, inspiring conversation on the plane ride had evaporated.

"Sorry, Nat. I didn't bring home any gifts for you guys," Tina remembered the pocket watch and clutched it firmly. "But I got one."

"What? From who?" Natalie asked.

Tina was surprised by her daughter's apparent interest. "The lady next to me on the plane gave me this neat old watch."

"An old watch?" Natalie asked sharply. "Who wants an old watch? And why'd she give it to *you*, anyway?"

"Natalie," Michael snapped without looking up. "Mind your tone."

THE SECRET WATCH

"Sorry Dad. Sorry Mom."

"Thanks, Honey," said Tina to Michael. She smiled softly. "Welcome home," she thought to herself. What a difference from Regina's homecoming.

She pressed the button on the shiny, silver pocket watch, but nothing happened. It wouldn't open. She tried it several times, but the watch would not open.

"Swell," Tina said under her breath. "I broke it."

Then she remembered the inscription: *"Help is a two-way street. Give. Receive."*

"Honey? I know it's getting late, but would you please take a look at this watch in the morning? It's lovely but I can't seem to get it to open. You're so much better at that sort of thing than I am."

"Sure thing," Michael replied.

Tina leaned back and opened her journal. The minutes ticked on. The car grew silent when Michael switched off the radio at the end of the evening sportscast. These late-night arrivals were always a source of stress and frustration for the family. It was a lot of work for Michael to pack the kids into the car and make the long trek to the airport. But Charlie was too much of a handful for Natalie and she was too old to tolerate a babysitter. Still, despite the hassle, Tina was grateful to see her whole family at the airport.

Tonight her thoughts touched briefly on the trip and her business struggles before settling comfortably on the curious old woman with the silver watch. She could not shake the feeling that Regina was somehow connected to the miracle she'd been looking for. She simply had no idea what it was or how Regina fit in.

"I could have used a new client or two. Instead, I've got this watch," Tina thought to herself.

Michael pulled into the driveway. Tina looked at the clock on the car radio. 11:57 "Almost tomorrow," she thought. Suddenly she realized how exhausted she was. She wanted to leave her luggage in the car but knew her husband had to work early the next day. The rest of the family piled out of the car and into the house. Tina started hefting her luggage.

"Honey?" Tina called to Michael.

Michael turned. He was carrying the sleeping Charlie over his shoulder like a sack of potatoes.

"After you put Charlie to bed could you please give me a hand with these? They're awfully heavy," she asked.

"Of course." Michael stepped into the house, moving directly to Charlie's bedroom. On the first trip inside, Tina brought her briefcase and handbag. She set the watch on the counter. Michael joined her in the driveway for the second trip into the house. He took both suitcases and sent her back in the house.

"I told you I'd get these. Why don't you get some sleep?" Michael said as he kissed her forehead. "You've had a long trip and we missed you. You can fill me in on the details tomorrow."

"Thank you," Tina replied, grateful. Sometimes she forgot that her husband was a really good guy.

She closed the trunk of the car and followed Michael back into the house, stopping in the kitchen to retrieve the watch from the counter. She looked at the clock on the stove. 12:10. Absent-mindedly, Tina pressed the button on the watch. This time, to her surprise, the cover sprang open. She looked at the face of the clock, comparing it to the clock on the stove.

"Twelve ten." Tina sighed. "It would have easily been twelve thirty if I hadn't asked Michael for help." She smiled and turned the watch to re-read the brilliant little inscription.

Standing shoeless in the kitchen her jaw dropped.

"Failure looks like the end of the road - until you make a new path."

Tina felt groggy and confused. This was not the inscription she remembered. Tina grabbed her journal and flipped to the last entry. She read: *"Help is a two-way street. Give. Receive."*

The inscription had changed. Either that, or her mind was playing tricks on her.

"That's what I thought. This is so weird!"

She rubbed her eyes and stared a long time at the inscription inside the cover of the watch. This time, though, she didn't dare close the cover. She took the watch and her journal with her to her room, placing them on the bedside nightstand.

THE SECRET WATCH

"I've got to get some sleep!" Tina said to herself as she dressed for bed. "I'm so tired I'm starting to see things! Or maybe I'm already dreaming."

LISA ROBBIN YOUNG

4. Your Priorities Revealed

"It is not enough to be busy, so are the ants. The question is, 'What are we busy about?'"
-- Henry David Thoreau

There was something about the Monday morning alarm that always seemed to come earlier - and louder - than those that followed during the rest of the week. Michael was up and out of the bedroom faster than she could say 'good morning,' so she didn't bother.

Actually, the routine made her smile. After fifteen years, there was a familiar rhythm to the morning: Michael liked to get up, shower and start his day before the rest of the house was stirring. Invariably, he'd wake Tina just before he left for work to make sure he got his good-bye kiss. Then she would roll back over and sleep until it was time to ready the kids for school. It was their little ritual to start the day.

This morning, however, after Michael headed for the shower, Tina couldn't go back to sleep. She sat upright in bed, grabbed her journal and fumbled around for the strange old watch. It was open, just as she had left it before bedtime. She held it up in the dim morning light and strained to read the inscription.

"Failure looks like the end of the road - until you make a new path."

"Good. Same as last night. Maybe I'm not losing it after all," Tina thought as she copied the inscription neatly into her journal. When she finished, she picked up the watch and examined it, scrutinizing the cover, running her fingers over the etched inscription.

"There's no way the inscription could change. It's engraved, for goodness sake," Tina exclaimed to herself. She ran her fingers over the entire face of the watch, the sides, even the fob, looking for some kind of clue, trap door, or projection screen.

THE SECRET WATCH

Anything that could explain the inscription change. She found nothing.

Just then, Michael came back into the room and she quickly closed the watch.

"Oh you got it to open?" Michael asked.

"Uh, yeah," she replied. Tina pressed the button on the top of the watch, but the watch once again refused to open.

"Uh, no," she said sheepishly, "I guess not."

"I'll take a look at it when I get home tonight," Michael replied.

"That's okay," Tina said, hastily. "I'm planning to call Regina - the lady who gave me the watch. I want to thank her again. Maybe there's some sort of secret to getting it open. I'm sure she'll shed some light on the situation."

"Great idea," Michael said. He leaned across the bed and kissed his wife before heading out for the day. "See you tonight."

"Yep. Have a good one, Hon. Drive carefully," Tina responded.

For a few minutes, Tina sat silently in her bed, holding the watch, trying to get a feel for exactly what was going on. No matter what she tried the watch simply would not open. She didn't want to break it so she placed it on her vanity and reluctantly continued her morning routine.

After last night's long drive from the airport, the kids were still sleepy which, thankfully for Tina, translated to fairly docile and easy to manage. Once she'd gotten their breakfast and sent them to greet the day, Tina turned her attention to work. Well, sort of. No matter how she tried to set her priorities, she was drawn back to the watch. She realized that nothing was going to happen until she satisfied at least some of her curiosity about the mysterious watch and its former owner.

She grabbed her phone and the card from inside her journal.

Tina glanced at the last note she had written.

"Failure looks like the end of the road - until you make a new path."

"Guess it's time to make a new path for myself," she said under her breath as she dialed the phone.

THE SECRET WATCH

"Hello. This is Marcus. How may I serve you?"

Tina was startled when her call was answered by a male voice. She re-checked the card in her hand.

Regina King, Business Consultant

"Um, hello. Sorry to disturb you. . . I seem to have dialed the wrong extension. I was actually looking for Mrs. King. My name is Tina and we met. . ."

"Oh, yes. Tina. Good to hear from you. I hoped you would call. Did you read today's inscription?"

"That's part of why I'm calling, actually. Well, that and I don't seem to know the secret to getting the watch to open. . . Wait. What do you mean 'today's inscription'?"

Marcus cut her off. "You're not doing anything wrong. That's part of what's so special about the watch. It only opens once a day, so it is important to read the inscription carefully."

Tina was surprised. "You know about this crazy watch?"

"Of course I do," Marcus replied, in a matter-of-fact tone. "Are you available to join Mother and me for lunch today? We'll explain further at that time."

Tina looked at her barren calendar. With only one project on the books, her schedule was pretty clear.

"That would be wonderful. What time? I'm intrigued by the story behind this watch," Tina replied, feeling both a bit nervous and quite excited. She noticed that the pounding in her chest was light -- not at all like what she'd been feeling at the conference.

"We'll be at The Summit House at noon. Will you join us?" Marcus asked.

Tina almost dropped the phone. She'd always wanted to go to The Summit House, but she wasn't entirely sure she would fit in there. Plus, she wasn't sure she could afford to dine at such a fancy establishment. Then, she remembered today's inscription, and decided to make a new path for herself.

"I'll be there with bells on!" Tina replied.

"Excellent. Although I'm not sure that 'bells' are exactly what The Summit House dress code would consider proper attire. I'll call George and have you added to the guest list," Marcus said. "You'll want to bring something for note taking. There is much for us to discuss."

"Okay. I'll see you at noon," Tina said brightly and hung up the phone.

Tina took a breath and looked in the mirror. Her frazzled morning appearance would never cut it at The Summit House.

The ancestral home of industrialist James Summit was situated in the center of a ten-acre plot of land. The elegant 19th century mansion was a sanctuary in the middle of the bustling city. James Summit eventually sold the home. It became a luxury restaurant and conference center. The Summit House was Detroit's most sought-after wedding and conference venue as well as a sort of a club for wealthy locals. Tina thought for a moment about what she might wear to such a fancy place.

"Oh crap! 'Proper attire?' What exactly does *that* mean? And how much time do I have?" Her thoughts turned to the crumpled mess of dress clothes in her still-packed suitcases. Rather than waste time beating herself up about the state of her luggage, she opened up her laptop and surfed over to The Summit House website, hoping it would spell out 'proper attire' in more detail. She sighed.

"'Smart Casual?' Huh? What the heck is that?" She read on. "'Dress with a jacket or coordinated pant-suit for ladies.' Okay. I think I have something that will work."

Tina ran to her bedroom and began flinging clothes onto the bed. In the back of her closet, she found it: classic, royal blue. It was an understated 2-piece suit-dress. One of the highest quality pieces of clothing left from her days in the corporate world. Tina liked it so much she couldn't bear to donate it, even though she hadn't expected to ever have a reason to wear it again.

"It'll be a miracle if this thing still fits," she said under her breath. "I haven't worn it in fifteen years."

Tina collected her undergarments, stockings and shoes and headed for the shower. Even though she wasn't sure why she was going, Tina wanted to be picture perfect for this meeting. It took her an hour to clean up, make-up, coif her hair and generally primp. She'd been working from home for so long she wasn't sure she even knew how to do it anymore. But Tina was determined to look her best. When she slipped into her dress it fit perfectly.

"Hello, old friend," she said with a smile as she greeted herself in the full-length mirror. "Long time, no see. It's time to step on to a new path. Shall we?"

Tina placed the silver watch in her purse and headed for the door.

LISA ROBBIN YOUNG

5. End of the Road?

"Failure is only the opportunity to begin again, only this time more wisely." -- Henry Ford

Tina was grateful that her husband had no idea where she was headed today: he'd probably blow a gasket. She looked in her wallet, praying that she wouldn't have to use her credit card to pay for lunch.

"Ten dollars? That should buy me a cup of tea. I hope."

Tina pulled up to the front of The Summit House and sighed again. Fortunately, the sign that said 'Valet Parking $5.00' was dwarfed by the magnificent setting: manicured lawn, topiary and the view of the city beyond. She thought of the watch and smiled.

"I certainly don't need to be reminded of the 'failure' part of that inscription, do I? I'm willing to step on to a new path, really I am. Besides, I can always eat when I get home," she thought.

Tina smiled as she handed the valet her ten-dollar bill.

"Keep the change," Tina grinned broadly as she took the claim check from the parking attendant.

"Thank you ma'am," the attendant said gratefully.

"I've always wanted to say that to someone," she thought as she ascended the front steps toward the door.

The large, antique oak and glass doors opened into a large, vaulted foyer. The room was almost as big as her eyes.

"Welcome to The Summit House," said the man behind the podium. "You have a reservation?"

"Holy smokes! The online photos do not do this place justice," she said, wide-eyed.

"Thank you, ma'am. A reservation?" The diminutive maitre d' was nonplussed.

"Oh, yes! Sorry. I'm here to see. . ."

"George, this is Tina. She's with Mother and me," Marcus interrupted as he approached the podium. Tina noticed that George stood a bit taller at the sound of Marcus' warm baritone voice.

"Yes, Mr. King. I have your guest on the list. Mrs. Williams, correct?" George asked, without even looking at the list.

"That's me," she beamed. "George, is it?"

"Yes, madam. George Entrega. At your service." He bowed slightly.

There was something in George's manner that Tina found captivating. Being attentive and welcoming was part of his job and, clearly, he was a master. But there was something that made Tina want to learn more. Dignity. Compassion. Charisma. She couldn't quite put her finger on what it was about the maitre d' of The Summit House that commanded so much attention and respect.

"Thank you. George. It's a real pleasure to meet you," Tina replied. "Hello, Marcus. Am I late?" She glanced at her wristwatch.

"No, no. You're right on time. Perfectly on time," Marcus smiled and directed her to the table where Regina was already seated. "We got here a bit early. Mother likes to be ready to receive her guests when they arrive."

George followed the pair back to the table and took Tina's coat, while Marcus pulled out a chair to seat her.

Tina had never been treated so nicely. "Thank you, Marcus. And you too, George. I feel like royalty!"

"My pleasure," George replied, again bowing slightly at the waist before he turned to go back to his post. Marcus smiled and came around the table to sit next to his mother.

Regina was wearing a simple tweed jacket with matching pants, elegant low-heeled pumps and a soft, powder blue silk blouse. The buttons on the blouse and shoes were pearly white and the way

THE SECRET WATCH

Regina was seated in the sun room caused the warm midday sun to glint off of them from time to time. Her handbag was made from creamy Italian leather, beautifully tooled with the initials 'RK' subtly adorning the flap. A slightly floppy hat with a powder blue band completed her ensemble.

Tina couldn't help but notice that the older woman's strength and confidence seemed to erase both Regina's years and the wheelchair. Tina found herself wishing for her friend's fashion sense and confidence: "Now and when I'm older," she thought.

"Hello, Dear One! I am so glad you were able to join us today."

"How could I refuse this invitation? I get to spend more time with you, maybe learn a little more at your feet. And Marcus, of course." Tina rambled a bit, revealing her nervousness. "The Summit House is amazing and I've never been here before. Oh, plus there's the watch, I have some questions. . ." Tina trailed off as she reached into her purse for the watch.

Regina smiled and took control of the conversation. "We're delighted you had courage enough to join us here and are both quite proud I must say. It has served us well."

Marcus nodded. "The Summit House . . . well, and the watch, too, I suppose," he smiled knowingly at his mother.

"Wait. You *own* . . . The Summit House . . . This is *your* place?" Tina asked.

Marcus nodded. Tina sat quietly trying to conceal her awe.

"Oh yes," Regina said. "The property has been in the family for years. When it was time for James Summit to relocate, my father made him an offer he couldn't refuse." She gestured toward the watch in Tina's hand.

The younger woman looked puzzled.

"Your father traded the watch to Mr. Summit? In exchange for this incredible property? Really?"

Regina nodded. Tina tried to piece it all together in her mind. She looked at the watch. While it looked old, perhaps from the 19th century, she couldn't imagine it to be worth more than a few thousand dollars at best. So why would a legendary industrial tycoon like James Summit trade valuable real estate -- including the dream home he had designed and built from the ground up -- for an old pocket watch that appeared to be worth far, far less?

"OK, now I'm really confused. This house had to be worth millions. Where did this watch come from? If your dad traded it to James Summit, how did you get it back? What kind of watch is this? It's obvious you two knew about the two different inscriptions. And what's the story on it anyway? Why all the secrecy? Why give it to me?" Tina's questions spilled out quickly, running into one another and sounding a bit stern. She was looking for answers and still wasn't completely sure about the questions.

"Tea, Dear One?" Regina artfully deflected Tina's insistent questions as George appeared with a tea cart. It, too, was elegantly dressed with lace and linens surrounding a sumptuous selection of scones and a variety of loose-leaf tea.

Tina was suddenly conscious of having spent her last ten dollars with the valet. She declined. "Um, no thanks, George."

Marcus was a perfect host. Sensing the cause of her discomfort, he spoke up. "Please have whatever you like, Tina. We invited you to lunch with us today. It's our pleasure to treat you to the full Summit House experience."

"Might I suggest the chamomile mint tea, Mrs. Williams? It pairs nicely with our signature cranberry scones," George said and began pouring for the table.

Tina seemed a bit guarded as she accepted a cup and thanked George, who was eager to make her feel welcome and at ease.

"It is always my pleasure to be of service," said George, smiling at Tina. He wheeled the tea cart out of the sun room and returned to his station.

Tina held the warm cup to her lips and inhaled the minty-sweet aroma of the tea. She sipped slowly, noticing and savoring the way it warmed her from the inside out. She'd almost forgotten about the watch.

"Now that we've all got some tea, I'll tell you the story," said Regina. Her face was still bright but Tina thought she noticed a hint of sadness as the older woman started to tell her how the watch had come to be hers.

"I was the oldest child of my family. When I was small, my father wasn't able to spend much time with us. Growing up, I thought of him as hard working but selfish. Every waking hour was spent working on one business idea or another. My mother's health was failing and the younger children became my responsibility. I had to grow up too quickly, I suppose."

Tina thought about her own family, and how hard she had been working lately.

"I remember when she died. I was so angry. My father wasn't there. He was off working, and it took me a long time to forgive him for how I felt he had mistreated both my mother and all of his children. Including me."

Marcus leaned in toward his mother and held her hand briefly. Regina stared into her teacup for a moment, as if to find an answer floating among the leaves. She looked up at Marcus and continued.

"One day, when I was seventeen, he came home with your watch. He claimed to have found it. None of us ever knew any different, but I was never comfortable with the story. A silver watch that was obviously valuable to someone would be missed. I was suspicious. For years, I believed my father had stolen it, and at the time I couldn't forgive him.

"But from that day forward, he was better. Refreshed. Attentive. He seemed nothing like the father I had known before. He became a successful businessman, which was also hard to believe after all the years of hardship and struggle we had faced. It didn't happen overnight, mind you. But he, himself, was a changed man. And it started the very same day he brought home that old watch. He called it his 'little good luck charm.'"

Tina looked at the little watch quizzically. Regina continued.

"I remained suspicious of everything he tried to do for me. I wouldn't even let him pay for my college education, which he tried repeatedly to do. He would send a payment to the bursar's office and I would deposit an equivalent sum in his bank account. We grew more and more distant as the years passed. It was a painful, bitter time for me. I wouldn't respond to his letters. I didn't even read them," Regina sighed heavily. "I wish now that I had."

Tina felt a heavy silence come over the table. She shifted her gaze to take in the room around her. Glasses and silver clinked. Other diners continued to chatter and laugh.

"So while I was busy being bitter, my father bought The Summit House, trading it for your watch. He left this house to me in his will, but I wanted nothing to do with it. I certainly didn't want to live in it," she said sadly, recalling the pain of their estrangement and the loss of her father.

"And then James Summit himself contacted me from beyond the grave," Regina said. "I am so often surprised by life's twists and turns."

Tina's eyes were wide.

Regina was amused by the expression on Tina's face. "Oh, no, Dear One. I don't mean some ghost came and haunted me, although, in a way I guess he did," Regina smiled a little and sipped her tea.

"On my thirtieth birthday -- which was more than a couple of years ago -- I received a package in the mail. It was from the Summit Family Foundation."

Tina smiled. "The watch?" she asked.

Marcus beamed. "Yes. And a letter."

Marcus reached down beside his mother and retrieved a leather portfolio. He passed it to Tina who opened it and began to skim over the letter as Regina continued.

"From his deathbed, James Summit wrote that letter to me. It talks about your watch and how it changed James into a different man. And that the same thing had happened to my father. See, as a young man James had worked hard, building his empire. His family didn't know him either. He goes on at some length about missed opportunities with his family and wishing he'd made better choices."

Tina looked up from the portfolio and listened intently to Regina's story.

"When my father offered James the watch in exchange for the property, it was as if he'd been given the chance to start fresh. James was a wealthy man by any measure and decided it was time to live the life he truly wanted. So my father got The Summit House and James retired to the country to enjoy his remaining days reacquainting himself with his family.

"My father wanted to prove to everyone that he had finally become the success he'd always known he could be. The Summit House was his legacy."

At that moment, George arrived with the soup and began ladling out three piping hot servings. He placed the breadbasket on the table and vanished almost as quickly as he had arrived.

"The house sat empty for about a year after my youngest sister graduated from college. I still wanted nothing to do with my father and his so-called legacy. At least not until I read that letter. James explained the special nature of the watch and how he felt compelled to give it to me so I could experience its unique qualities for myself. He also invited me to open my heart and visit the house again, but I was still too bitter. Fortunately, my husband was far more forgiving than I was and we visited here. He saw enormous potential for this restaurant and, as I was pregnant with Marcus at the time, I was in no position to argue," Regina smiled.

Tina stirred her soup, entranced by Regina and her story. "So then you opened the watch?"

"Not at first. It wasn't until years later, when Marcus was being mischievous that I was reunited with your watch. It was in the bottom of my jewelry box and my little boy was rummaging where he didn't belong."

She shot Marcus a mock-stern look, mimicking the one she had used so many years ago. "I believe he was about five at the time. The restaurant was humming along nicely and my husband was busy managing it."

"I remember that day so clearly. You were very upset with me, Mother," Marcus chuckled.

"Rightly so!" Regina teased, feigning indignance. Then she softened, looking deeply into her son's eyes. "The watch opened as I took it from you. You asked me to read it to you." Then, turning to Tina, said, "The inscription was the first one. . . the one you must have seen last night, Tina."

"Help is a two-way street. Give. Receive," Tina said.

"Yes, exactly," Regina smiled and nodded. "And I read it to Marcus that day, thinking it was a very odd inscription for a watch. I let him play with it, since I had no use for it. And, as little boys are wont to do, he left it lying on the dining room table. I found it the next morning, and the inscription was completely changed."

"Failure looks like the end of the road - until you make a new path," Tina beamed.

"And Mother was about as flummoxed as you sounded on the phone, Tina," Marcus laughed.

"Of course I was puzzled! So I dug out that old letter from James Summit. According to the accounts of both James and my father the watch only opens once a day. Each time it opens a new inscription appears."

"And it only opens a certain number of times. As far as we can tell, the longest it has ever spoken to anyone is sixty days," said Marcus.

"That's right, Dear Ones," said Regina. "When it has opened sixty times, it will not open again for you."

Regina began to eat her soup. Marcus spread butter on his scone.

"So why me? I mean, you could give it to Marcus or his children," Tina looked troubled and confused.

"Don't you worry, Tina," Regina smiled reassuringly. "When I saw your attitude on the plane, I wasn't so sure. I had no desire to sit next to a sourpuss on what would most likely be the last flight of my life. But with a little time and attention, you came around."

Tina sat, eyes wide.

"When it has finished with you," Regina continued, "I mean when you've read all the inscriptions the watch has for you . . . well, then you'll understand. Take your time. Each new inscription builds on the last. Don't rush it, and as I said last night, whatever you do, do *not* sell it."

"Oh, I won't, you can count on that!" Tina answered brightly. "But why can't you just tell me?"

"Learning these lessons for yourself is part of the journey," Marcus replied.

"Fair enough," Tina smiled.

"Now, Let's eat!" Regina exclaimed.

6. Family First

"You don't choose your family. They are God's gift to you, as you are to them." -- Desmond Tutu

Tina returned home refreshed, with a renewed sense of confidence. She also felt a bit of pressure to live up to the legacy of the strange silver watch with which she had been entrusted. Still, her curiosity led her to wonder what significance it must hold.

"If the rest of the inscriptions are as instructional as these, I'm bound to see some success." Tina said under her breath as she pulled the mail out of the box. She sighed at the stack of incoming bills. "I just hope it happens fast enough."

Tina spent the rest of the day mapping out goals and objectives for her business for the next sixty days. There would be sixty important messages coming her way. She decided it was important to make space in her life to accommodate this new learning. Tina wanted to make the most of the time she'd have with her new "business partner" -- the lovely antique watch now hanging elegantly from a chain around her neck.

She placed the stack of bills on the kitchen counter and went to work. It was relatively simple to map out the next couple of months, since she didn't currently have much in the way of client workload. A small project from a long-term client would be finished in the next couple of weeks, opening up a few hours in Tina's day, just in time to start preparing for the enormous family Thanksgiving dinner that she and Michael hosted each year.

Adding some projected meetings and lunches with Marcus and Regina, the calendar still looked pretty thin. Tina decided to schedule specific times each day to follow up with contacts from the conference.

Completing the plan for the next two months, she turned to her daily distraction. In her email inbox, Tina saw a message from Natalie reminding her about today's after school chess club pick-up. She glanced at the clock.

"It's already time to leave. So much for getting anything accomplished today," Tina said with a sigh. She grabbed her keys, hopped in the car and headed for the elementary school to collect Charlie before going over to the high school.

The ride was pretty uneventful. Natalie was plugged in to her music for the entire ride. Charlie chattered about his day at school while Tina mumbled the obligatory, "Oh really? That's nice, dear," to her son. As usual, her mind was a million miles away. For once, though, Tina wasn't focused on paying bills, but instead on this strange little watch and what her life might become now that she had it in her possession.

"Mommy?" Charlie said. "You're not listening to me."

"I know, buddy. That's wonderful," Tina replied. Then, realizing what Charlie had said, she stopped herself, apologized and continued the ride home with a little more attention to her children.

When Michael arrived, dinner was on the table and everyone was ready to eat. He hung his coat, kissed his lovely wife, and greeted his children as they all sat and began devouring the meal.

"I'll take a look at that watch after dinner, Honey," Michael said to Tina.

"Oh, no need." Tina tried to sound casual and unconcerned. "Regina said it's supposed to do that."

Michael looked up at her and, for the first time since he'd arrived at home, really saw Tina. "New dress?"

"No. It's been in the back of the closet for a few years now," Tina sighed. "I went to The Summit House to meet Regina and her son for lunch today."

Now it was Michael's turn for wide eyes. Natalie stopped eating and almost dropped her fork when she heard the words 'Summit House' cross her mother's lips.

"Wow! Really Mom? The Summit House? That place is super-fancy. You met the watch lady at The Summit House?" Natalie sounded a little impressed.

Michael was a little more cautious.

"What did THAT do to the budget?" he asked with tension in his voice.

"I paid the valet ten dollars. Everything else was covered by Regina and Marcus."

Michael seemed relieved. "You must have made quite an impression during that plane ride."

"Help is a two-way street. Give. Receive," Tina replied, smiling. "I like them. And I have a feeling they can teach me some things that will be good for my business. Regina and Marcus have invited me to meet with them at least once a week for the next couple of months and I'm making the space in my work calendar to be there."

Charlie smiled and tried to sound important. "Mommy, you look beautiful. Will you wear that blue dress all the time? You look like a princess."

Tina turned to the other end of the table and smiled at her innocent little boy. "Thank you, Honey. I'm sure I can find something besides this dress to wear all the time," she said without missing a beat. In the back of her mind, though, she was already trying to figure out what to do about her wardrobe dilemma.

After dinner, Michael spent time with the children while Tina turned the bedroom closet upside down and inside out, looking for alternative clothing choices for next week's luncheon with Regina and Marcus. Surely she couldn't wear the same dress again next week. They would notice. And yet, in the end, her closet quest turned up little beyond a white hat, gloves and a silk scarf she had inherited from her grandmother.

"It will have to do," Tina said quietly, taking the blue dress to the laundry room to wash it -- gentle cycle, air dry -- to keep it in the best possible condition.

When she returned from the laundry room, the bedroom had been transformed. All the clothes were back where they belonged and Michael was reading the last of a chapter in his favorite book before he went to sleep.

"The kids are asleep," Michael said, without looking up.

"Oh my word," Tina was surprised. "What time is it?"

"Ten thirty. I'm ready to sleep," Michael replied, closing his book.

THE SECRET WATCH

"Thank you for cleaning up my mess, Michael," Tina said graciously. "Sorry I'm a little preoccupied."

Michael smiled. "You're welcome. I love you. Even when you're a little preoccupied."

Tina momentarily debated staying up until midnight to open the watch, but decided that sleep would be a better course of action.

"Goodnight, Honey," Tina whispered, turning off the light.

"G'night," Michael yawned as he closed his eyes and began to drift.

LISA ROBBIN YOUNG

7. Priority One

*"Things which matter most must never be at
the mercy of things which matter least."*
-- Johann Wolfgang von Goethe

The week after that first luncheon was almost
excruciating for Tina. Every morning, she hopped
out of bed with her husband to sneak a peek at her
watch before starting the day. She felt like a little
child with Christmas presents under the tree --
barely able to contain her excitement while waiting
to read the new message waiting inside.

Michael wasn't sure what to make of his wife's new
early rising trend, but it was nice to spend some
quiet time with her before he left the house for the

day. He decided to enjoy it for as long as it lasted, however long that might be.

While Michael showered, Tina would spend her first few waking moments with her journal: writing down inscriptions, making notes about what they meant to her and jotting ideas for action steps she could implement during her day. Some were easier to understand and act on than others.

"What's 'Priority One' today? Do it first."

This came fairly easily to Tina. She was good at prioritizing and, most days, felt quite able to determine the 'Number One' priority for both her life and her business. It's just that her laundry list of action items was usually longer than she could ever accomplish in a single day. Tina quickly learned that whittling down her list of to-do's made her 'todays' more productive.

But the day she woke up to:

"You might as well have fun with it!"

was a little tougher.

Tina could always find more work: a floor that needed cleaning, a shelf that needed dusting, or a contact that needed calling. Her children needed rides here and there, help with homework and she wanted to be attentive to Michael. By the end of the day, she was often exhausted and cranky. Fun felt like a luxury . . . an 'extra' Tina did not feel she had the time, interest or energy to consider.

Mentally grumbling about the 'stupid watch' and its 'crazy ideas' Tina remembered part of her previous conversation with Regina. The older woman had spoken about her resistance to certain ideas along the way.

"For me it was the rift within the family . . . the harder I tried to avoid it, the bigger it seemed to get. At the time I thought the watch had gotten stuck on messages about family and forgiveness. It seemed like the same message was being paraphrased day after day. I guess that's the way it is with most of the important things we need to learn, Dear One," her mentor had told her.

So, with Regina's words ringing in her ears, Tina began finding ways to make her long, daily to-do lists more pleasant. She started by playing energizing music whenever she was cleaning and even danced a bit while mopping floors. Charlie and Natalie caught her dancing in the kitchen one morning before school and fell out laughing at their mother's awkwardness. Tina laughed and danced anyway.

"Make time for fun"

the watch read the next morning.

"Apparently I need this fun idea more than I thought," said Tina to herself. Upon taking a deep breath to help think about it, she noticed that her jaw was tightly clenched.

In a rare moment of unselfconscious spontaneity, Tina let out a loud growl. "GRRRRRRRR!!!"

Michael was starting to get used to the odd little blips that were quickly becoming part of the couple's morning routine. He raised an eyebrow in her direction.

"Hey, it's better than howling at the moon, right?" she giggled, bear-hugging her husband while offering up another playful growl and some nibbles on his neck.

When, a few moments later, their daily good-bye kiss was clearly more passionate than usual, Tina realized that -- especially with the more difficult inscriptions -- the rewards far outweighed her resistance.

"I could get used to this 'enjoying my day' stuff," Tina said glancing out the window at her husband pulling out of the driveway. She began to look for small ways to add what she called 'frivolous moments,' her little daily pit stops of joy. She literally stopped to smell flowers or listen to her favorite music -- without always working along. At first, Tina found it difficult to stop working long enough to enjoy herself so she started making little notes in her calendar. She actually scheduled time to have fun.

A few days into the inscriptions, Tina began creating new routines to help herself practice these new concepts. She was surprised to find herself approaching her calls and her work with fresh eyes and a renewed spirit. She enjoyed her work more and more throughout the day. Even her client remarked at her new found joie d' vivre.

One night after dinner, Michael and the children were shocked to find Tina pulling out board games from the closet.

"Let's play a game," she said with delight.

Her family was stunned.

"Who are you and what have you done with my wife?" Michael asked, half cautious, half joking.

"Honey, we need to make time for fun in our lives and I would really like it if we all played together tonight," Tina pressed, determined to have an enjoyable time with her family.

And they did.

"Find quiet stillness daily."

Even more challenging than putting some fun in her day, Tina struggled with finding quiet time. Charlie always seemed to know when she was awake and could barely wait to greet her. She rarely completed her morning journal entries without an interruption or three from someone in the house. But after a couple of days, Tina found that if she delayed her email distraction by just a few minutes, she was able to clear her mind and find an oasis of stillness.

"Take a walk - it clears the mind, refreshes the body, renews the spirit."

THE SECRET WATCH

"OK," said Tina to the lovely little watch. "At no point did anyone warn me that these were going to get more difficult."

That was probably a good thing. Exercising was even more of a challenge than stillness. Tina wasn't in the best of shape, but she could still keep up with Charlie, so she didn't feel the need for much other physical activity. And, for the most part, Tina was able to keep her weight under control by watching what she ate. Finding time to exercise was simply not on her agenda.

The phrase 'use it or lose it' popped into her mind. She didn't want to lose the messages from the watch so she decided to take its latest suggestion as seriously as possible.

Tina began simply -- by taking a walk from her front door to the mailbox instead of waiting for Michael to get home and bring in the mail. It did not take long for the trip to the mailbox to become a walk through the garden and eventually around the block.

"Expand your vocabulary."

"Finally, one I like." Tina loved new words and found she could involve her kids in this challenge as well. Vocabulary building became a family activity; Natalie and Charlie soon began trying to stump their mother with a new word each day. Even Michael got into the spirit, bringing home new vocabulary words from work, challenging the rest of the family to broaden their linguistic horizons by including some scientific terminology.

They made a game of it, challenging one another to use the new words in context. They were all taken aback one day when Charlie began to explain the metamorphosis of butterflies in exacting detail, using some of the vocabulary he had learned.

"They hafta turn into goo and reorganize their chromosomes before they can fly. They stop bein' a caterpillar and start changin' into a bufferfly," Charlie beamed. "And you can't help 'em when they're struggling out of the chrysalis or they won't never fly. They have to make their wing muscles strong." Charlie smiled brightly. "Chromosomes, caterpillar, and chrysalis. That's three new words that start with the letter 'c', Mommy!"

Michael and Tina puffed with pride. Even Natalie sounded impressed when she offered a "Good job, Squirt!" to her younger brother.

But the hardest lesson of the week was the inscription that greeted Tina the morning of her next scheduled luncheon with Marcus and Regina.

"Faith: small stepping stones build tall towers."

Tina pondered the inscription. She was self-conscious about returning to The Summit House wearing the exact same outfit.

"Well, I'll just have faith that the hat and gloves look so great no one will notice my dress," Tina said to herself as she stepped out the door for the drive to The Summit House.

LISA ROBBIN YOUNG

8. *Small Stones, Tall Towers*

"Be faithful in small things because it is in them that
your strength lies." -- Mother Teresa

Walking up the steps to the front of The Summit
House, George was waiting to greet her. He
promptly left his station and saw to her coat as fast
as she could walk through the door.

"Thank you, George," Tina said with a smile.

"Lovely hat, Madam," George replied with all
seriousness.

"Really?" Tina inquired. "You don't think it's too
old?"

George smiled knowingly. "It's a perfect fit for both the occasion and the location."

Tina felt a bit of relief. She noticed Marcus approaching. She crossed the foyer, greeting him with an extended hand.

"Marcus," she said in her most professional tone.

"Tina," Marcus replied with a tone that was almost as polished as his shoes. "Mother and I are looking forward to your report."

"Indeed," Tina smiled as they crossed into the sun room, where Regina waited for them.

Tina was instantly taken aback when she saw Regina. The older woman was wearing the same powder blue silk blouse and coordinating tweed ensemble that she'd worn the week before.

"Good afternoon, Dear One," Regina smiled, setting Tina instantly at ease. "You look splendid in that hat."

"Thank you, Regina," Tina said awkwardly. "It's an heirloom and I rarely get a chance to wear it."

THE SECRET WATCH

"You wear it well, Dear One," Regina reassured her.

Marcus seated Tina at the table and the three dug in to the most recent secrets revealed by the watch.

"The most difficult concept for me so far was 'quiet stillness.' Well, at least until I saw this morning's message," Tina said.

"Do tell," Marcus encouraged as he poured a second cup of tea. "What was today's inscription?"

"Don't you already know?" Tina asked.

"From what we can tell, not all of the inscriptions of the Secret Watch appear in the same order," Marcus replied.

"Yes," Regina chimed in. "They seem to have a mind of their own, appearing according to the need of the owner. As a matter of fact, it would seem that the harder lessons tend to come earlier. Perhaps because we need more time to work through them."

Marcus and Regina exchanged knowing glances. Tina looked a bit puzzled, but recited the day's inscription aloud: *"Faith: small stepping stones build tall towers."*

Regina clapped her gloved hands together in delight. "That's one of my favorites! Tell me your reaction," the older woman urged.

"Well," Tina stammered. "I suppose if I want to build a successful business -- or anything for that matter -- I need to take lots of small steps. Building brick by brick."

"Precisely," Marcus beamed. "And you can't always know exactly what will happen before you lay the first brick."

"Or the next one," Tina said.

"Or the one after that," Regina said, regaining control of the conversation. "That's the act of faith -- the willingness to even lay a brick in the first place. And that first brick ultimately becomes the cornerstone of a tall tower."

"Like coming here today," Tina said aloud, surprising herself as well as her hosts. She gasped and offered apologies to Marcus and Regina.

"Why are you apologizing? It took courage for you to return to a setting where you very obviously feel out of place," Regina reassured her.

"You can say that again," Tina smiled, a bit relieved.

"But why do you feel out of place here, Tina?" Regina pressed.

"Well, I see all the beautiful fancy plates and clothes and people . . . There's not much about me that feels very fancy," Tina sighed.

"And still you came. Why?" Regina was relentless.

"Because you invited me," Tina stammered. "I trust that you and Marcus will treat me well."

"Really?" Regina smiled.

"Uh-oh. Did I make a bad assumption?" Tina's stomach started churning. Her uneasiness was apparent on her face.

"Relax, Dear One," Regina relented. "The point I'm trying to make is that you had just enough faith in Marcus and me that you were willing to drive out here to join us again. It certainly wasn't the lure of a free meal that gave you the courage to face all the discomfort and awkwardness you're feeling right now, correct?"

Tina shifted in her seat. Highlighting her awkwardness only made her feel more uncomfortable.

"Correct," she said, trying to relax. "I came because I believe you've given me a special opportunity: a gift. I'm grateful and I want to make the most of it."

"So if nothing else, you have faith in the opportunity. In the gift," Regina affirmed.

"Well, yes, I suppose so," Tina thought for a moment, as she picked up her tea cup and stared into the bowl, much as Regina had done the week before. She felt as if she wasn't stating her case properly.

"I also have faith that, given the right information, I can lay my own bricks and build my own tower -- with or without the Secret Watch," said Tina.

Marcus and Regina looked at each other with pride.

"Didn't you just say this was a difficult concept? You must have gotten up VERY early this morning," Regina teased with a warm smile. Tina felt her confidence returning. In that moment, she knew that Marcus and Regina were not strangers anymore. They were fast becoming the friends and mentors who might just help her turn her business around.

"Well, do we want to move on to the issue of quiet stillness?" Tina teased as they continued their luncheon, enjoying the bright, warm sun streaming through the windows.

LISA ROBBIN YOUNG

9. Work v. Play

"The bow too tensely strung is easily broken."
--Publilius Syrus

On the drive home, Tina took a mental count of the ways in which her life was already changing -- even if her bank balance hadn't yet budged. She held out hope that all these positive steps would ultimately translate into more than the spare change rolling around at the bottom of her handbag.

She glanced at the fuel gauge on the car and sent up a flare prayer asking that she make it home before running out of gas. Just then, her cell phone rang. When she saw it was The Summit House she maneuvered her car to the side of the road.

"This is Tina," she answered quickly, after moving safely out of traffic.

"Mrs. Williams? It's George from The Summit House," came the voice on the other end. "You dropped a glove on your way out and you were in such a hurry I was unable to catch you."

Tina sat stumped for a moment. If she drove back, she'd definitely run out of gas before getting home. Before she could decide how to respond George offered to hold the glove at his station until her return the following week.

"Yes, thank you. That would be a big help," Tina replied, relieved. "Thank you for your kindness. I'll see you next week."

"Truly, my pleasure, ma'am," George said, as she hung up the phone and continued her drive home.

Tina made a mental note to add one more little change to the list she was keeping in her journal: she had faith that she would attend next week's luncheon.

As she pulled into the drive, Tina's mind began to race looking for ideas to bring in at least enough money to put gas in her car. Thankfully, her husband got paid in a few days, but if she was going to continue these forays to The Summit House she felt responsible for covering the travel expenses.

With only a few of hours before the kids were due home from school, Tina pulled out her journal and the stack of business cards she had collected at the conference. One by one, she jotted down names, professions, and any details she could remember from their conversations. She used the cards to create a mind map. Within an hour, there was a rich web of data at her fingertips.

She stood up, admiring her labor: one part art plus one part strategy, hopefully adding up to new revenues. Soon.

"Well, I've got the data. Now what to do with it?" Tina said to herself.

Then, standing above her handiwork, it struck her. So many of the business cards looked the same. In fact, many of them seemed to blend right in to the white background of the paper. Tina was inspired and sorted the most mundane cards into one pile and set the remaining cards aside.

Slowly, she matched her notes about each contact with their cards. Tina began to notice patterns. On the back of one particularly boring card, she had scrawled, "Loves music. Doesn't feel like a bean-counter." On another, she'd written, "Creative and fun. Hates her boring job. Wants to do something artistic."

Then it hit her: many of those boring cards were given to her by some of the most interesting people she met. The plainest cards were from five of the six people she spent the most time with at the event.

"I guess it's time to put this faith thing into practice," Tina said, as she cleared the table of all but those five cards. She spread out her materials and began to draw.

So intense was her focus that two hours ticked by before she even noticed the noises of her children. Not only were they home -- they were fighting.

"Mom! Charlie took my headphones!" Natalie shrieked.

"Did not!" Charlie retorted, in an equally shrill tone. "You left them on the table!"

THE SECRET WATCH

The bickering wouldn't stop, and Tina had no patience. She stepped into the hallway outside her office. This time the shrieking voice was hers.

"Oh my goodness! Can't you guys get along for just ten minutes? You've only just walked in the door and already you're fighting with each other! Where's your father?" Tina demanded.

From behind her, Michael's calm, steady voice silenced the shrieking. "I'm right here. We've been home for over an hour now. You must be working pretty hard in there."

Tina's face turned as red as her lipstick. She shrunk a little as she realized what had just happened.

"Um, yes. And, oh! I'm so sorry. I shouldn't have yelled. I'm sorry, Honey," Tina turned to her children. "I'm really sorry, kids. I guess I completely lost track of time. I didn't even hear you until just now. I didn't know you were home."

"That fancy watch is a piece of junk if it can't tell time," Charlie snapped.

"Charlie!" Michael said in a reprimanding tone.

"Sorry, Dad. Sorry, Mom," Charlie said.

"Charlie," Tina replied. "This watch is special to me because it was a gift, not because it can tell time."

"Well, alls I know is that you said you lost track of time and didn't know we were here. That doesn't sound very special to me!" Charlie replied.

Tina chuckled. "I suppose not. But it's not an alarm clock, so we can't blame the watch. Blame me. I was focused on a project and completely in the zone. Let me change my perspective, because I had it backwards: you guys were so quiet and well-behaved, I didn't even know you were here."

Charlie started to smile. Natalie was unmoved.

"Mom, you're wearing your princess dress again," Charlie observed. "Does that mean you went to the fancy people's house again?"

Natalie chuckled. "It's called The Summit House, squirt. And they don't live there. It's a restaurant."

"Actually," Tina said gently. "Regina's family *did* once live there. She owns The Summit House."

Natalie's eyes were huge. "Mom! Really? You know rich people?"

Michael and Tina laughed out loud.

"Okay, kids. Mom's working. We need to give her some peace and quiet." Michael grinned at his wife as he herded the children away from Tina's office. "We can take over dinner if that would help you," he said.

The look on Tina's face was all the response he needed.

"Let's go, small folks," said Michael.

Charlie cheered, Natalie groaned and the kids migrated to the kitchen to help their father with dinner.

LISA ROBBIN YOUNG

10. The Antidote

I have learned over the years that when one's mind is
made up, this diminishes fear. --Rosa Parks

For the next few days, Tina worked diligently in her
office crafting designs for prospective clients and
the hours seemed to fly by. Then she contacted
four of the five individuals from the conference,
and while they appreciated her efforts, they were
not in the market for a new design.

Instead of feeling defeated, she was surprised to
find she enjoyed using those conversations to catch
up with her new colleagues. She asked each of
them what they were working on and how she might
be able to help with referrals. She asked each of

them for referrals as well. Tina walked away from each call with more information, but nothing to add to her checkbook. With only one contact left, her optimism was starting to fade.

Fortunately, she received the final payment from her existing client a few days before her next scheduled meeting with Marcus and Regina. Not only did it relieve the pressure for a few weeks, it also enabled her to visit an upscale consignment shop to find another outfit suitable for The Summit House. She picked out a well-constructed silver grey suit that fit her perfectly. The blue satin blouse she found added just the right splash of color to the ensemble. At first, she thought it looked a little too much like something Regina might wear.

"There are worse things in the world than looking like a well-respected, wealthy woman," Tina chuckled to herself. "Besides, I look great!"

She took the outfit home and hung it on her closet door for Monday's luncheon.

Early Monday morning, Tina reviewed her notes from the two previous luncheons. She wanted to be prepared for whatever lessons Marcus and Regina had in store for her later that day. She also reviewed the last several inscriptions and her notes about what each had meant to her. Finally she noted the changes she had experienced in her life and business.

Her mind began to wander. Once again Tina found herself seeing patterns. She moved into her office and, quickly jotting abbreviations on separate slips of paper, started to arrange them as she had the business cards a few days earlier. She grouped the inscriptions, attitude shifts and other lessons around different topics. There were inscriptions that focused on money issues:

"Your financial house needs a strong foundation."

and some that were focused on family:

"Prioritize your family to show they are valued."

But there were other ideas, too. Like taking better care of yourself:

"Take a walk - it clears the mind, refreshes the body, renews the spirit."

and even enjoying life:

"Make time for fun."

Tina found herself most troubled by the inscriptions about faith. She stared at the three inscriptions that had given her the most difficulty over the past two weeks:

"Faith: small stepping stones build tall towers."

"Failure looks like the end of the road until you make a new path."

"Fear is a poison. Faith is the antidote."

It was almost as if this watch was challenging the strength of her resolve. Her confidence was shaky and here she was, creating designs for people on spec -- just hoping to be hired. So far four of the five people had said, "Thanks, but no thanks."

"That's an 80% failure rate," she said to herself. "No wonder I'm so uncertain about this faith thing."

Tina shook off the cold feeling in the pit of her stomach and got the kids off to school. She decided that there was nothing to lose by reaching out to her remaining contact. But first she decided to get ready for her lunch date with Regina and Marcus.

"I might as well have fun with it," Tina reminded herself of an earlier inscription. She cranked up the tunes while she showered, put on her 'new' outfit and makeup. Looking at her own polished reflection staring back from the mirror she felt more energized and alive.

Tina's dark hair framed her face and the blue top electrified her smile. Her grey suit looked as if it was tailored to fit her exact measurements. She looked like a woman who meant business.

"I'm ready!" she said, dancing over to turn off the tunes so she could give full attention to her phone call.

She dialed Jason Jenkins, the gregarious and creative red-headed corporate trainer with the bland, boring business card.

Tina remembered how well they hit it off at the conference. Jason was effervescent, bordering on effusive when he shook her hand. They lunched together two of the three days of the conference.

Of all the potential leads, Jason was the one she knew best. His demeanor was so outgoing, so welcoming, Tina was convinced that if anyone would hire her, it was Jason. His cards were downright plain and too traditional for his charming personality. She was confident that her design would not only turn his head, but could possibly make him a client for life. At least that's what she hoped as she took a deep breath and waited for his voice mail to pick up.

"This is Jason, how's the sun shining in your world today?" came a lively voice from the other end of the line.

"Um, hello, Jason. My name is Tina Williams, and we met at the conference two weeks ago. . ."

"Oh yes, of course!" Jason sounded excited. "I got your email. Thanks so much for re-connecting. I kept your card from the conference, and I had been meaning to call you, but we've been swamped here. I'm really glad you called."

"Really?" Tina said, sounding hopeful.

"Yes," Jason replied. "When I first saw your card at the conference, I wished that I had something so creative and well-designed. I loved the one you sent me. It was brilliant and exactly what I want for myself. I really felt like you captured my personality on a little piece of card stock. You have a great eye. It's really fantastic work, Tina."

Tina's heart leaped in her chest.

"Unfortunately, until I get out on my own, there's not much I can do. All employee cards are handled at the corporate level. . ."

"Oh." Tina felt her heart sink and struggled to stay focused on Jason's words.

". . .but you might be able to help on another project. I'm in dire need of some design help. Our staff designer took a new assignment at another company. I've got a presentation that's due. . . oh my. . ." He trailed off.

"Oh my . . . what?" Tina asked, sounding a bit desperate.

"Well, it looks as if the presentation is due in ten days," Jason said, embarrassed. "I'm sorry to have gotten your hopes up. I mean, doing a business card design in a few weeks is one thing. I wouldn't ask you to do an entire project in only ten days' time. I'm sure you must be booked."

"Well," Tina countered. "What's the scope of the project? I can't promise miracles, but I still may be able to lend a hand," she said.

Jason breathed a sigh of relief. "Really? Do you have time to talk about it now?"

Tina stifled the urge to squeal.

"I've got about an hour right now before I have to leave for a meeting," she said.

"Are you kidding? You are a lifesaver! I knew connecting with you at that conference was a smart move!" Jason exclaimed.

Tina took a deep breath, looked up to the ceiling, mouthed a big 'thank you' and then kissed the precious watch hanging from her neck. She listened intently as Jason explained the purpose of the presentation, the target audience, the company's needs and some of the obstacles they were facing with cleaning up the original designer's work.

"So really, you're not starting from scratch; I know that sometimes it's harder to pick up where a designer left off than it is to just start all over. Do you really think you can make space in your schedule to pull it off?" Jason asked.

"Well, until I see the files, I can't know for certain, but I think we can work out something that will meet your deadline and fit my schedule," Tina said.

She knew, except for the big family Thanksgiving dinner this weekend, her calendar was bare. She swallowed hard and presented her terms.

"And, since you're a new client, I'll waive my normal rush fee for a project of this scope. As soon as you send the deposit and upload the files, we can get down to work." Tina said.

"Brilliant!" Jason exclaimed. "We'll process payment this afternoon and upload the files to you immediately so that you have everything you need to get started." He paused. "I'm so glad we connected!"

"Me too," Tina replied. "I look forward to getting started! Have a great afternoon."

As she hung up the phone, she whispered under her breath. "You have no idea how glad I am. No idea at all."

LISA ROBBIN YOUNG

11. *Good Enough Rarely Is*

"The quality of a leader is reflected in the standards they set for themselves." -- Ray Kroc

With a bit more spring in her step, Tina dashed off to The Summit House for lunch. On the way out the door she looked at herself in the mirror, once again admiring the new outfit. Starting the car, she noticed and appreciated the full tank of gas, and for once, enjoyed the drive. She pulled into valet parking. Her cell phone notified her of incoming messages: not only had Jason's deposit payment been completed, the files were waiting in her inbox.

She almost strutted up the front steps to George's podium.

"Good afternoon, George," Tina sang confidently.

"Good afternoon, Mrs. Williams. What a lovely outfit," George replied. "And here is your glove."

"Thank you, George."

Tina looked around for Marcus and Regina, but did not see them.

"You'll be dining alone today," said George. "Mr. King sends his regrets and told me to give this to you." He handed her an envelope.

Tina looked a bit startled.

"No worries, Mrs. Williams. We'll take good care of you," said the maitre d'. "And, as a close friend of the family, your name has been added to the house account," George reassured her.

Realizing that Tina did not know how to respond George added, "Your meals here are complimentary."

"Close friend?" Tina sounded puzzled, but decided not to press her luck. "Thank you George. Did

Marcus say why they would not be in attendance today?"

She did her best to sound unruffled.

"No, ma'am," George replied. "I was only given this envelope for you. Please follow me, and I'll escort you to your seat."

Tina was taken to a private booth with a spectacular view of the south lawn. There, she placed her order and stared at the envelope, half afraid to open it.

Suddenly, it dawned on Tina that she hadn't opened the watch yet. It was the first day in weeks she hadn't rushed to see what new lesson was in store for her. She looked again at the envelope, unsure of what was waiting inside and opted instead to open the watch.

She removed the watch from around her neck, and depressed the button on the top of the fob. The watch opened, revealing another new inscription.

"Good enough rarely is. Not enough usually is."

Tina jotted down the peculiar phrase in her journal and puzzled over the meaning of it. At first, all her insecurities started to surface. She wondered why she was still sitting here, alone, in this beautiful setting. She had felt out of place from her very first visit -- even though she tried hard to fit in. Perhaps that was the problem. Maybe she was trying too hard. All her 'not enough' self-talk was having its way with her when she realized George was standing at the table with the service cart and her soup.

"Are you well, ma'am?" George asked. "You look uncomfortable. Is the sun too bright? Would you like me to adjust the window shades?"

"What?" was all that Tina could muster.

"The sun, ma'am. Is it too bright?"

"Oh. No. I'm just pondering this inscription."

Tina recited the inscription to George.

"Is that Mrs. King's old watch?" George said marveling at the intricacy of the cover. "I thought she gave that to Mr. King many years ago."

Tina looked up at George and then at the watch. "Yes. It was Marcus' watch. They gave it to me a few weeks ago."

"They must think very highly of you," he said.

Tina felt even more uncomfortable and shifted in her seat.

"George, what do you know about this watch?" Tina asked, trying to pull the attention off of herself.

"Very little, I'm afraid. I only know that it has been in the family for years and was passed on from Mrs. King's father, and that Mrs. King then passed it to her son. You must be quite like family if they've passed it to you instead of to one of Mr. King's own children."

"Yes," Tina said. "I am very blessed."

"Yes, ma'am," George said. He glanced down at Tina's writing. "I can tell you what I know about the inscription if you'd like."

Tina sat straighter in the chair. "I'd like that very much."

"I remember the day I first heard it." George recalled. "It was my very first week on the job here. Mrs. King had booked the entire facility for her son's high school graduation party. We were all on our toes. And Mr. King -- that is, the senior Mr.

King -- was inspecting everyone and reminding us how important it was to keep things running smoothly, but not to obsess. He wanted us to do our very best."

Tina looked up at George, who seemed somehow taller.

"He had called us all together a few minutes before the guests were scheduled to arrive. He told us 'good enough rarely is but not enough usually is.' He explained that doing the minimum is rarely enough, and that we should always strive to do our best in every situation.

"Then he reminded us that all we can do is our best, and to expect more than that from ourselves would always lead us to feeling as if even our best efforts were not enough. Those words have stuck with me my entire life."

George smiled. "I'm sorry, ma'am. I didn't mean to go on such. Your soup is probably cold now."

Tina waved off his objections. "You and my soup are perfectly fine. Thank you for your insight. I'm sure Mr. King's advice will stick with me as well. The Summit House has a real treasure in you, George."

"Yes, ma'am," George blushed. He served her soup and returned to his post.

It wouldn't have mattered if Tina's soup was cold because she barely touched it. Her mind was wrapped around the 'not enoughs' that had been holding her back in life. She knew that her own limiting beliefs were keeping her from the success she so deeply desired. She also acknowledged that these tiny inscriptions had helped her shake something loose in her mind -- a new perspective, perhaps -- that paved the way to a more empowered future.

Once her meal was presented, she thanked George and picked up the envelope.

"Why am I being so foolish? Marcus and Regina have been nothing but wonderful to me. I must be faithful to them," Tina thought to herself and hesitantly opened the envelope.

Tina,

If our faith in you is on target, you are enjoying your soup right now. My apologies for the short notice: George and the rest of the staff will take excellent care of you. Mother was not well this evening and asked me to make sure we met as scheduled on Monday. I'm sure you can understand my desire to be with her this Thanksgiving week -- even if she might put up a fuss. Please allow this letter to serve as our 'lesson' for the week.

By now, you have no doubt noticed a pattern in the inscriptions. Mother calls them her Five Key Areas of Success:

- *Faith (spiritual and personal)*
- *Family (by blood or not)*
- *Fitness (mental and physical)*
- *Fortune (personal and business)*
- *Freedom (making choices about the stuff of life)*

Each of the inscriptions fits into one of these categories and, in the spirit of the Secret Watch, often in more than one area. As you look back over the inscriptions you've read so far, you should be able to see these themes developing.

At the moment, my priority is 'Family.' Should you ever have to make a similar choice, I pray you will be able to do so as easily as I did today.

My apologies for not being with you today in person. Enjoy your meal. Please have dessert -- and hopefully we can meet again soon. Call me to confirm you've received this.

Fondly,

-Marcus

Tina folded the letter neatly and placed it on the table.

"Is everything alright, Mrs. Williams?" George had been watching her for several minutes, looking for indications of distress.

"I'm fine, thanks George. When did Marcus leave this letter with you?"

"Last week when they were in for dinner," George replied. "Mr. King made it clear I was not to call you but to deliver the letter when you arrived today. He said it was some sort of test."

"I see," Tina said a bit absently still staring at the letter.

"Did you pass?" George asked, trying not to sound too eager.

"I'm not sure," Tina admitted. "I hope so. I guess time will tell."

She picked up her phone and dialed Marcus. There was no answer.

"Marcus, this is Tina. I got your letter and hope Regina is feeling better. Please give her my best. I don't know what else to say, but if I am able to help in any way, please let me know."

Tina disconnected the call and stared at her meal. She picked at it quietly before asking that the rest of her meal be boxed. She still didn't feel comfortable eating here without Marcus and Regina.

"Are you sure everything is all right, ma'am?" George persisted.

Tina paused for a moment, looking first to George, then to the rest of the patrons nearby. They were socializing and carrying on as if nothing had changed. These were some of the most prominent members of the community and they all seemed to be going about their business as if it were another routine day for them.

Tina, on the other hand, had undergone a radical shift. In that moment she realized no one was staring at the young business woman eating alone. No one was looking at her second hand clothes or judging her appearance. They were, in fact, quite engrossed in their own conversations, meals and pleasantries, and in no way thinking of her.

Tina chuckled softly to herself at how ridiculous it had been to believe that anyone there would be watching her every move. She realized her own 'not enough' self-talk was being washed away. Tina finally knew she could belong here. She smiled, knowing Regina and Marcus had probably planned it that way.

"On second thought, George, I'll stay. What would you recommend for dessert?"

George smiled and suggested a tartlet with lemon creme sauce. Tina sat by herself, enjoying both the view and the meal, wondering if she should ring Marcus again. She decided against it.

"Regina probably needs her rest." Tina thought to herself. "I just hope everything is going to be okay."

She finished her meal and rose to leave. George motioned to the valet to bring her car around. As Tina walked past the podium, George stopped her. "Your car will be ready in a moment, Mrs. Williams."

"Thank you," Tina replied half-heartedly.

"Certainly, ma'am," he replied. "I trust you are going to the house, now? Please offer my well wishes to Mrs. King."

"The house? Um. . ." Tina thought for a moment. She had no idea where Regina and Marcus actually lived, but tried her best to maintain the appearance of close friend of the family.

"I don't know how to get there from here," Tina replied.

George smiled and drew her a map. She took it willingly and quickly hugged him as her car pulled up in front of the building.

"Thank you, George! You are a gem!"

12. Friends As Family

"Friends are relatives you make for yourself."
--Eustache Deschamps

Prominent Detroiters, from Henry Ford to Willie Horton, and later Berry Gordy Jr., have called the city's Boston-Edison section home. From the Italian Renaissance 'Motown Mansion' to the understated two-story colonials: every home was unique and colorful. The wide, grassy strip running down the middle of the largest streets gave the feeling of a lush park nestled between a series of one-way streets.

Pulling on to Boston Boulevard, Tina slowed to a crawl. The esplanade was so wide, she at first thought she had dead-ended into a park. Then, on the other side of the street, she saw the house: 700 Boston Boulevard.

The immense structure was a sprawling, elegant English manor constructed from light-colored field stone. It seemed completely right-sized amid the other mansions on the street. Driving past homes so rich in history left Tina wondering again how she'd ever managed to befriend people who seemed so unlike her. This time, though, she managed to silence the negative self-talk almost immediately.

Tina pulled up to the gate and pressed the button for the intercom. Robert, the driver, recognized her immediately and opened the gate from the other side.

"Welcome to The Manor," he said. "Mr. King is inside with his mother. Please go in through the kitchen door." He gestured to the back of the house. "It's open."

"Thank you. Roger, is it?" Tina asked, unsure if she remembered correctly.

"It's Robert, ma'am," he smiled.

"I apologize, Robert. Thank you. I won't make that mistake again!" Tina smiled warmly and ushered herself indoors.

The kitchen felt like an intimate space; if not for the side-by-side stoves and vaulted ceiling it might have looked like any other kitchen. Straight ahead, Tina could see a small dining room and a modest table, stacked high with file folders and papers. To the right was a butler's pantry, easily twice the size of the kitchen, with another stove, sink and service area.

She moved through the pantry to the main dining room where her mouth gaped at the sight of a crystal chandelier, marble fireplace and dining table with seating for fourteen. As she crossed to the opposite end of the dining room, she heard footsteps in the foyer. She closed her mouth, straightened her dress, and continued through to the main entry where Marcus was descending a massive wooden staircase. Nearing the bottom of the stairs he smiled broadly. Tina stood motionless, unsure of what to say or even why she was there.

"You came!" Marcus' voice boomed through the foyer, causing the suit of armor to rattle.

"Um, yes," Tina replied timidly. "I felt I had to."

Marcus looked at her approvingly. "Sometimes friends are as family."

"Yes!" Tina said, surprised and relieved. "That was yesterday's inscription. I wasn't sure what it meant until. . . well. . . right now," she laughed.

"Welcome, Tina," Marcus said, opening his arms wide. "Mother was betting you would come. She's upstairs. Let me take you," he said.

With some trepidation, Tina followed Marcus up the winding staircase. Treading softly, she took it all in: the large painting on the wall, floor-to-ceiling mirror, over-sized grandfather clock in the corner at the turn of the stairs.

"How is she?" Tina asked in a whisper.

"Her health has been failing for a while now," Marcus sighed as they continued their ascent. "I've been trying to bring her home for months, but she insisted that she was fine on her own, handling business as usual. She's always been a traveler, so asking her to slow down is like trying to stop a speeding bullet."

She smiled at the image of Regina as a speeding bullet. "I imagine asking Regina to do anything she doesn't want to do would be problematic ... for the one doing the asking," Tina replied.

"Yes, well, she took a turn for the worse when she was out visiting one of our properties in Minneapolis. She ended up in the hospital for several weeks before they okayed her return to Michigan," Marcus replied as they came to the top of the stairs. He stopped and turned to Tina.

"The doctor insisted on a wheelchair for the flight home, which infuriated her. Mother is a strong woman, and asking for help has always been one of her opportunities for growth. She's been using the wheelchair ever since." His face saddened. "She's relentless, though. Insisted on going out much more than I'd like. At dinner last week, she nearly collapsed. That's when she took to her bed. The doctors say it's only a matter of time," he said.

Tina's eyes welled up. Marcus patted her shoulder and resumed their walk down the hall decked with framed photos of every size, shape and subject. There were children, teens and adults in a wide range of poses with an equal variety of backdrops. The Eiffel Tower. A beach. Mount Rushmore. A playground. Tina wanted to ask about each of the photos but her curiosity felt far less important than seeing Regina.

"These are the kids and grandkids, of course," Marcus said as he gestured to the photos on the wall. "My kids are all grown now. Here's a picture of Mother and me from more than a couple of years ago. It's my favorite."

He pointed to an ornate, gilded frame hanging just outside the bedroom door. Regina's voice, softer than usual, came from beyond the door, "Are you showing off that old thing again?"

Marcus gently pulled the frame from the wall and opened the door to his mother's bedroom. Regina was sitting up, surrounded by at least half a dozen fluffy pillows. She was, of course, fully clothed and ready for company. Looking slightly tired and sounding short of breath were the only signs of her failing health.

"I couldn't resist, Mother," Marcus replied sheepishly. "I cherish this picture almost as much as I cherish you."

"Sweet talker," Regina cooed. "He always knows just what to say."

Tina looked over the photo in the gilded frame. A young man, perhaps in his twenties stood with his arm around a much younger-looking Regina. They were standing in front of the huge fireplace at The Summit House. Both of them looked incredibly happy.

"It is a lovely photo, Regina," Tina said. "When was it taken?"

"I had just graduated college," Marcus replied. "We celebrated with a private luncheon at The Summit House. Just the two of us. Not a customer in the house . . . just Mother and me," he said quietly.

Tina offered the frame back to Marcus. In the corner of the picture, Tina thought she saw a familiar profile. "Is that George?" she asked.

Marcus stood gazing at the photo, recalling every detail of the day in his mind. "Yes. I believe it is. Funny. I remember the first time I met him, when I graduated from high school, but I don't think I ever noticed him in this picture until now."

"Well, you were a bit distracted that day, Son," Regina reminded him.

"True, Mother," Marcus recalled. He turned to Tina. "It was when she first shared the Secret Watch with me. It's a day I'll never forget," Marcus said, smiling.

He looked over at his mother, who appeared to be breathing more easily. He continued, "It was also the day I was put in charge of The Summit House. Over time, I have assumed responsibility for most of the family holdings."

"And it was the day he met Milagra," said Regina a bit smugly.

"Who?" Tina asked.

"Milagra was our table server that day," Marcus smiled. "She took that photo," he said, wistfully. "Her name means 'miracle' and she certainly was for me. She was the most beautiful woman I had ever seen. At first, I thought she was a bit delicate, like fine crystal, but she proved me wrong. She had a fiery spirit and a real zest for life. We played volleyball together all summer. She made me feel like a champion. We were inseparable. . ."

"They got married that same fall," Regina chirped.

"Really?" Tina asked. "That was fast, wasn't it?"

"I suppose," answered Marcus. "But important events have a way of changing time."

"I still think she's the real reason you cherish that picture so much," Regina poked at her son.

"She's one of them, Mother. And you know it," Marcus smiled.

"I know, Son. And I'm grateful," Regina smiled.

Tina looked on as mother and son shared a tender moment. Regina broke the silence.

"How was your week, Dear One?" she asked.

"Well, let's see," Tina answered. "I got your letter, obviously, and you were right. I did start seeing patterns. I like your Five Key Areas of Success and can see how the inscriptions fall into categories. . . and that some really DO fit more than one category," she said. "For a while I thought that the concept of 'fun' was going to be one of the categories, but I see how it fits into several others."

The proud mentor smiled broadly. "That's wonderful." Regina pressed on. "Why are you here today, Dear One?"

123

Tina stood awkwardly for a moment. It was not a question she'd anticipated and the old insecurity came rushing back. For an instant she thought she might have overstepped their relationship by coming to her mentor's home. Her mind quickly sorted through several responses before she decided to ignore it and allow her heart to speak up.

"I'm here today because sometimes friends are as family. And because I've learned a little something about faith," the younger woman answered confidently.

Marcus and Regina looked at each other in pleasant surprise.

"Really?" Regina said. "Tell me more," she said brightly.

Tina recounted her plan to design business card samples. She told them about the way stepping out in faith had already brought her a lucrative account, an appreciative client and a project with the deposit already paid.

"My husband doesn't even know yet here I am, telling you both. I'm thrilled. It's a big leap forward for me. Scary, but definitely rewarding," Tina beamed.

Marcus flashed a smile at his mother. "Exactly what we were hoping to hear," he said.

"Oh?" Tina asked, feeling a bit out of the loop. "Actually, I've been kind of hoping the two of you would tell me why I'm here. Frankly, this is all still a bit hard to believe," said Tina.

"What do you mean?" Regina asked, a knowing look on her face.

"I am grateful to you both, really I am. But in truth, I'm a stranger. You gave me this crazy watch, took precious time from your lives and invited me to these meetings to share what I'm learning from the watch -- but you already know everything there is to know about it. You've had it for years, shared it with your family, and yet you're still asking questions about its secrets. Then you turn around and invite me into your home during Thanksgiving week when you could be focusing on your own family. I don't get it," Tina said.

Suddenly she realized her enthusiasm had amplified her voice. Tina looked from Regina to Marcus and back. They both seemed a bit amused by her display.

Tina giggled uncomfortably. "Sorry. I guess I just have a hard time believing that total strangers would be so nice to me," she said.

"There are several problems with your assessment, Tina. You're usually so much more astute." Regina shook her head in mock sternness. "First of all, we have not been asking questions about the watch."

Tina looked puzzled. "What do you mean?"

Regina continued, sounding stronger. "You are correct: we already know all we can about the watch and its secrets. In fact, we still know much more about it than you do. We haven't been asking about the watch. We are asking about you: Tina Williams."

Tina looked up from her shoes long enough to realize that Regina and Marcus were serious. She swallowed hard.

Regina continued.

"Secondly, you *were* a stranger. Then we became friends. You helped me during our flight, asking for nothing in return. Your generosity inspired me. I wanted to reciprocate. I knew you would find value in the watch, but I wanted to be sure you would implement the lessons. The best way to do that was to invite you in. Sometimes friends are as family, as you know," said Regina more softly.

"Yes, I am learning that," Tina replied sheepishly.

"Do you remember how I came to have the watch?" Regina asked.

Tina thought back to their first luncheon together and the story about Regina's father, their years of estrangement and how the watch brought them back together.

"Yes, ma'am," Tina replied.

"You don't give a watch like this to just anyone. For years, recipients have been painstakingly selected. As Marcus rose in the ranks of the company, each of his children has had it for a time."

Marcus continued. "My grandchildren aren't yet old enough to appreciate it. Besides, their parents are all well-versed in the lessons of the watch. Mother and I have been looking for the right person for quite some time now. We felt it was important to extend its reach and be sure it was in good hands . . . before . . . she . . ." Marcus trailed off.

"Before I die," Regina finished bluntly. "It's only a matter of time and the watch must always be passed on to the right person. We've been searching for several years now. You'll learn about that when it gives your final inscription."

"It won't open for just anyone," Marcus continued.

"You mean we have to be worthy or something?" Tina struggled to understand all of the nuances they were trying to share with her.

"Sort of," Marcus replied. "You'll understand when you read the final inscription."

"Can't you just tell me now?" Tina pressed.

"Of course we could," Regina interrupted, trying to soothe them both. "But where would the adventure be? So far you've managed to have faith in the process. Hasn't that been working for you?" Regina asked.

Tina smiled.

"Faith," she sighed. "Looks like this is a lesson that is going to last all week long -- at least. Act in faith. Trust the process."

"Well done!" Regina smiled and breathed deeply. "Faith is the foundation. Believe in yourself, in the process. The more quickly we heed the messages of the Secret Watch, the sooner we see success. For each of us the lessons may come in a different order, but they are always from The Five Key Areas of Success. You will understand everything if you continue to trust the process."

She let out a heavy sigh and motioned to Marcus for assistance. Marcus provided an arm for his mother to lean on. She climbed out of her bed and moved slowly toward Tina.

"Fair enough," Tina offered. "I'll do my best. Good enough rarely is, and not enough usually is. Right?"

Regina stood a bit straighter and embraced her friend. She whispered softly in Tina's ear.

"Well done, Dear One! Now if you will excuse me, I have doctor's orders requiring me to rest. It's exasperating, but I do have a stack of reading to catch up on." Regina motioned toward the foot-high pile of books on her night stand.

"Of course." Tina giggled softly, remembering the speeding bullet image from earlier. "I'll be on my way." Tina excused herself from the room.

"Not so fast, Tina!" Regina commanded in a semi-dramatic tone. "Marcus will see you out in a moment. There's one more thing before you leave." Regina threw a wink toward Marcus.

"Certainly," Tina replied, smiling. "Shall I wait in the hall and let you have some privacy?"

"That will be just fine," Regina replied.

13. Believe In Something

"Those who don't believe in magic will
never find it." -- Roald Dahl

Marcus closed the door to the master suite and
escorted Tina back down the stairs to the great
hall, leading her back through the dining room to
the small kitchen.

"Please wait here," he said.

Marcus walked into the smaller dining room and
pulled an overstuffed notebook off the top of one
of the piles. He walked back to Tina and handed it
to her.

"Careful," he said. "There are a lot of loose papers
in there."

Tina looked at Marcus with a quizzical expression on her face.

"This will help you to work through the next few weeks. Before she got sick, Mother started to organize letters from family members and others who have owned the watch at various times," said Marcus.

Opening the notebook with care, Tina saw dozens of envelopes, addressed in longhand and some by computer. There was a letter from James Summit and one from Marcus.

"All of these people have had the watch?" Tina asked.

Marcus nodded. "I expect Mother's health to continue to decline over the holidays. I plan to be here with her, enjoying our time together and helping her to make final arrangements. Please continue to be our guest at The Summit House, explore the notebook and reach out to us whenever you have questions. I will join you if I'm able, but you'll know that if I'm not there, this is why." Marcus gestured overhead to where his mother was now resting.

"I understand," Tina nodded and turned toward the door.

"Tina," Marcus called to her.

"Yes, Marcus?"

"Mother really thinks the world of you," he said.

"Thank you, Marcus. I hope I don't let her down," she said.

"I don't think you ever could, Tina."

The next few weeks were hectic. After returning from The Manor, Tina dove headlong into Jason's design project. She finished ahead of schedule and on budget, delighting her new client so much that he offered her three additional projects. They would carry her financially through at least the first quarter of the coming year.

As the week continued, preparations for her family's Thanksgiving dinner seemed nearly effortless. Everyone -- including Natalie and Charlie -- pitched in to make it a success.

By now Michael was familiar with the secrets of the mysterious watch. While his scientific brain still didn't understand it, neither did he look a gift horse in the mouth. Both Michael and Tina began to reinforce its lessons with their children. Things were turning around for them. Not just for the family, but financially as well.

The money from Jason's project allowed Tina and Michael to breathe easier about paying the bills. They took the opportunity to closely examine their finances. Neither was surprised when the watch offered encouragement and inspiration in the form of two powerful inscriptions:

"Money is not character... but always reveals it."

"Money can divide your heart and your home if you let it."

They sorted through wants and needs before creating a budget that included significant lines for giving, investing and saving. It felt odd . . . and very, very right. Tina felt less and less compelled to jump out of bed and read the inscriptions first thing in the morning. Instead she chose to spend that time reflecting, grounding and centering herself for the day. She also made a point to spend more time with Michael -- something he was certainly pleased about.

Still, life wasn't perfect. Although the kids liked to see their parents spending more time alone together, it was an adjustment and there were growing pains.

The Secret Watch reminded Tina that:

> *"Children aren't the only ones who need boundaries"*

and to:

> *"Honor family time."*

> *"Work when you're working. Play when you're playing."*

"Wow. Another timely message as usual," she said aloud as she opened the watch at the end of her work day. She wrote down the inscription, organized her notes and closed her laptop. "What good is making more money if I spend all my time locked away in the office?"

She turned the watch over in her hand and said to herself, "I think these lessons about what really matters are finally starting to sink in." She turned the light off in her office.

14. Believe In You

"Every man must do two things alone; he must do his own believing and his own dying." -- Martin Luther

With Christmas approaching, Tina still maintained her weekly Summit House appointment. In addition, she occasionally traveled there to work on the notebook Marcus had provided. Its contents seemed to make more sense when she was seated at the The Summit House, soaking up the ambiance. It was as if she could step directly into the stories of James Summit, Marcus, and even Regina's father.

George was faithfully ready to assist her, although as the weeks went on, she didn't require much help. Without realizing it, Tina had begun to navigate the facility with ease, as if she belonged there. She came to know each of the staff by name and, of course, always looked forward to talking with George.

Marcus was only able to join her for one more lunch and then only long enough to pass her a package.

"You don't have to open it right now. It's the menu and notes from several meetings about our branding," Marcus said. "We're considering some changes to the look and feel of things at The Summit House and since you're a designer, Mother thought we should ask you."

"I'd be honored," Tina replied. "It's a great opportunity for me to repay some of your kindness."

Marcus shook his head. "Mother and I won't hear of it! You have to earn your keep. Send us a proposal and a budget and we'll set a date for your bid presentation."

With that, he turned and headed for the door.

Tina sat dumbfounded for a moment. "A budget and proposal?" Tina thought to herself. "For a menu?"

Tina opened the large brown accordion file, pulled out one of the file folders and flipped through it for a few moments before her salad arrived. It wasn't just a menu -- it was an entire brand overhaul for The Summit House -- right down to the logo. Ideas were coming quickly, but Marcus had given her no indication of what they might be looking for in a new design.

Momentarily frantic, Tina considered following Marcus to the lobby. The entire overhaul of a company's branding is a major undertaking. She noticed her hand shaking as she examined the menu.

Then it hit her. She knew why Marcus and Regina had insisted she continue coming to The Summit House in their absence. It wasn't for a free meal. They weren't just being kind. It was an opportunity to fully experience the facility and its amenities so she could meld that knowledge with her creativity to get this job done.

"Well, duh, Dear One!" Tina said to herself.

When her salad arrived, she looked at it carefully before taking the first bite. She knew it would be fresh and delicious -- the beautiful presentation and the icy cold plate made it even better. Attention to detail was a hallmark of what made The Summit House one of the most talked about establishments of its kind. Michigan's wealthy and elite consistently chose The Summit House because of the quality of the experience. Attention to even the tiniest of details was an important part of that.

She thoroughly surveyed her surroundings: the staff, the decor and the clientele. She took it all in, taking care to pay particular attention to even the smallest details: polished brass flue handle on the fireplace, perfectly folded red pocket squares in the vests of the servers, and spotless windows.

The more she noticed, the more excited she became, until finally she had to share it with her husband. When the voice mail picked up, she spoke so rapidly she wasn't sure if Michael could even understand what she was saying. She was far too excited to care.

"Honey?" Tina said after the beep, "Call me when you get this. I think we're about to have a very merry Christmas AND a Happy New Year!"

Although the approaching holidays had Tina already feeling a bit of time pressure, the addition of a really big project somehow made everything feel just right.

She took to heart all of the lessons from the Secret Watch, reviewing her journal twice a day to maintain both balance and focus. As a result, her business continued to grow, and her family fully enjoyed their holiday season.

Despite all of that, as the days ticked by, Tina felt more nervous than ever. Not only was she preparing one of the most important proposals of her career, she was doing it for someone she had grown to love. She hoped the quality of her work would reflect the admiration and gratitude she had developed for Marcus and Regina King.

LISA ROBBIN YOUNG

15. Character & Integrity

"If you want to know what a man's like, take a good
look at how he treats his inferiors,
not his equals." -- J.K. Rowling

Two days after Christmas, Tina appeared at the
Summit House as scheduled. She wore a brand new
outfit purchased for the special presentation.
Simple. Elegant. Classy. It reminded her of
something Regina might wear. "Maybe I really AM
starting to follow in my mentor's footsteps," she
thought as she quickly checked herself in the hall
mirror.

George met her in the foyer, a weighty brown
envelope in hand. Tina approached him with a big
smile.

"Hello, George! I see you got my package," Tina said, extending her hand in greeting.
George shook it enthusiastically. "Yes, Mrs. Williams. I'm honored that you included me in this," he said, gesturing to the great hall where Tina had set the presentation.

"How could I not?" she asked. Tina was sincere. "No one knows as much about this place as you. The clients, all the staff . . . everyone knows George Entrega."

He beamed. "Yes ma'am. Still, I feel honored," he said.

He escorted Tina to the great hall. As they entered, she motioned to George, indicating the front row. "I've saved you a seat of honor, right up front, George. You were an invaluable help in this project," Tina said.

George took his seat in the front row next to Marcus. The several dozen remaining seats were occupied by shift leaders for each of the service teams, the chief valet and several regular patrons.

"Good afternoon, George. I can hardly wait to see what Mrs. Williams has in store for us," Marcus said. He motioned to the cameraman; everything was ready for the simulcast to Regina's hospital bed. Although her health was fading faster every day the old woman had insisted on being part of the event. Much to the chagrin of the nursing staff, Regina King had finally embraced a little technology.

When the cameraman gave Tina the thumbs up, she walked to the podium at the front of the room.

"Good afternoon and thank you all for coming. I've asked you here today for several reasons. First, and most important, I want to say 'thank you' for your input and generosity throughout the past few weeks. Whether with service, hospitality, time or ideas, every person in this room has contributed to the plan and design of the new concepts you are about to see.

"The Summit House has a long and rich history pre-dating the fine dining experience you've all come to know and expect. As you all know, this place has come to represent so much more to the community than a place to eat.

"The pedigree of excellence at the Summit House has led to many great success stories -- some of which you may know and some that will remain forever private."

Tina cast a knowing glance at Marcus, who beamed.

"This is a family business and each of you has graciously welcomed me as its newest member," Tina said, looking out at the faces of the staff. "I've not only learned about the history and heritage of the Summit House, but also about each one of you: your struggles and triumphs, and of course, your families."

Tina turned to face the camera.

"Regina and Marcus have quite a legacy here, and it is, in large part, a result of the hard work, loyalty -- and love -- of the people in this room. Every day your efforts to inspire your teams create an environment and an experience that makes every patron feel special. Important. Your actions let them know just how much they matter."

THE SECRET WATCH

She smiled broadly and turned to the long-term
patrons in the room. Most of them were nodding
their agreement.

"Our honored guests are a vital part of the Summit
House story. Week after month after year -- inviting
your families, friends and colleagues to share meals
and milestones on the grounds . . . you are the
reason we do what we do."

Tina continued her remarks as she moved to the
storyboard.

"When Marcus and Regina asked me here a few
short weeks ago, I had no idea what I was getting
myself into. I've lived in this city my whole life but
never imagined I'd see the inside of the Summit
House. I thought it was too fancy for me. The Kings
had other ideas. For weeks, they kept bringing me
back to enjoy the wonderful food, impeccable
service and lovely surroundings." She paused and
turned to George.

"Mr. Entrega, how you ever put up with me, I
haven't a clue. I was so full of fear and you were so
very kind and helpful. Thank you," Tina smiled
warmly.

147

George blushed. "My pleasure, entirely."

"Secondly, I've asked you all here to bear witness. When I finally learned I could be of service to Regina and Marcus, I took the charge very seriously. Yet, what I've documented on this board is nothing more than capturing the story that you have so graciously shared with me. I asked you here so that you could be among the first to see the results of your efforts.

"In each row, there is a large brown envelope. Please open it now. Take a look at the mock-up of what I hope will become the new menu for the Summit House. Please pass them around to the people seated near you."

Tina removed the drape from the storyboard. George, Marcus and the entire audience opened their envelopes.

Marcus studied the rich, brown leather portfolio that opened to reveal crisp ivory stock with woodcut-styled images of staff and patrons nestled amongst the menu selections.

"I wanted the menu to have a look of traditional elegance, but to be modern enough to reflect the character that gives the Summit House its distinctive flair. As you turn the pages, you may recognize yourselves, your events and your memories," said Tina.

The cameraman moved in close on the storyboard so Regina could have a closer look. The audience murmured positive comments. Marcus looked at Tina and nodded approvingly.

"You'll also notice the logo has been refreshed. I've taken the same font that has come to represent the Summit House and framed it as if it were hanging -- welcoming -- over the entry of an historic home," said Tina.

"It's exactly what we hoped for," Regina interrupted, her voice a bit hoarse. "Oh my, Dear One, you've done very well. Very well, indeed," said her mentor from the screen.

"Thank you, Regina," Tina replied. She turned to face the screen, effectively shutting out everyone else in the room. "That means the world to me."

The technology seemed to disappear as the two women looked fondly at one another.

Marcus crossed to the storyboard, took the microphone from Tina and addressed the audience. "Ladies and gentlemen, honored guests, Mrs. Williams. Thank you so much for being here today."

"I agree with Mother: the design you've just seen is exactly the 'feel' we wanted to capture. We're delighted with the time and attention you've taken with the project, Tina," he said. "You've told the story like . . . well . . . as only a member of the family could."

Tina blushed, looked at her shoes and forced a smile.

"Mother and I will take a closer look at your design. We'd also like to consider input from our team members and honored guests. George, if you'll pass around the comment cards. Friends, you'll find a drop box for those cards at either end of the refreshment table. Please enjoy the buffet . . . and kindly leave your remarks with us before you leave this afternoon. We truly want our new look to reflect what the Summit House ultimately represents . . . and Tina's right, nobody knows that better than the people in this room. Thank you all again for coming."

The audience broke into applause and congratulations. Marcus declared the meeting adjourned and ushered the guests to the sun room for a reception.

LISA ROBBIN YOUNG

16. Honor Family Time

"I sustain myself with the love of family."
-- Maya Angelou

"Congratulations on a job well-done, Mrs. Williams," said Marcus as he offered Tina a congratulatory drink and a hug.

"Thank you, Marcus." Tina replied. "What are the next steps in your decision process?"

"Well, I'll take the comment cards back to Mother -- at her insistence. Then, we will look at what we have from other potential designers and make our decision."

"But Regina's in the hospital. She needs her rest and. . ."

"You know Mother, Tina. She's got the nurses in a tizzy right now over the video link in her room. She's hell bent on staying active in one way or another for as long as she possibly can."

"I understand." Tina smiled. Again, the image of Regina as a speeding bullet popped into her mind.

"Now, if you'll excuse me, I'm going to be with Mother," Marcus said. "She insisted that I be here but I'd rather be at the hospital."

Tina smiled.

"Oh, sorry. I realize how that must have sounded. Your presentation was wonderful, Tina. Really," Marcus said apologetically.

"Why are you still here?" Tina teased. "Give Regina my love and prayers."

"Of course," Marcus gave her a quick hug and departed.

"Mrs. Williams," George said, approaching from behind.

"Yes, George. What is it?"

"One of the patrons wants to speak with you about your presentation. I think he may want to hire you!" George said, excited.

Tina straightened her jacket and rejoined the reception.

17. Don't Wait

"Do not take life too seriously. You will never get out of it alive." -- Elbert Hubbard

That evening, Tina's phone rang. She and her family had gotten into the habit of not answering the phone during dinner, but something told Tina to check the caller ID anyway. The call was coming from the hospital.

"I need to take this, Honey," Tina explained. "It's probably about Regina."

"Tell the rich lady we said 'hi' and that we are praying for her to get all better!" Charlie exclaimed.

Tina smiled. Her husband nodded and she took the phone into the living room away from prying ears.

"This is Tina," she said.

"Tina, it's Marcus. Can you come to the hospital tonight?" he asked.

"Well, yeah. Sure. Um. Is everything alright?" Tina stammered. She was hoping this call wouldn't come.

"Mother insisted I call. She wants to see you face-to-face. I think that should be tonight if at all possible."

"I'm on my way."

Tina hung up the phone and walked slowly back to the kitchen and her family. She returned the phone on the charger on the kitchen counter.

"I need to go to the hospital tonight, Michael," Tina said softly.

"Regina?" Michael asked.

"Yes. Marcus says she's asking for me."

"Sometimes friends are as family, right Tina?"
Michael asked with encouragement.

Tina looked at her family. So much had changed for
them in the past few weeks. She hardly recognized
them -- or herself for that matter. She brightened
and did her best to smile cheerfully.

"Yes, Michael. Exactly."

Tina hugged her children, kissed her husband, and
grabbed a cookie for the road.

The hospital wasn't far but the drive felt like an
eternity. Tina glanced at the clock in the car every
other minute, which only increased the anxiety she
was feeling. She did not handle death well, and
spending time in hospitals was part of that. It made
her really nervous.

Fifteen minutes after getting the call from Marcus,
Tina pulled her car into the visitor lot. She stroked
the silver watch hanging from her neck and headed
inside.

Despite the attempt to be as warm and welcoming
as possible, the hospital's antiseptic atmosphere set

Tina on edge. The clerk at the information desk was cordial, almost cheery. He directed Tina to the elevators on the north side of the building, where she could find her way to Regina's room on the tenth floor.

She checked her reflection in the polished stainless steel elevator wall, adjusted her winter coat and debated whether or not to take it off. She glanced at the other passengers in the elevator. One by one, they exited on different floors. The elevator was quiet. Tina could hear her thoughts rattling around in her head:

"What am I doing here?" Tina demanded of herself. "This is a family matter, and no matter how much I want to pretend otherwise, I'm not part of the King family. What good could it possibly do to have me in the hospital while Regina is dying? I HATE hospitals. I REALLY don't want to do this! WHY am I doing this?"

The elevator chimed. The doors opened to the tenth floor. Tina felt her feet moving on their own accord. She stepped out of the elevator. The doors closed behind her.

"No turning back now," she thought to herself.

"May I help you?" came a voice from the nurses' station. Tina spotted the top of someone's head behind the desk.

"Um, yes. Regina King's room?" Tina said, regaining her focus.

"Room 1024. Follow the yellow line around the corner to your left." The nurse said, without looking up.

"Thank you."

Tina turned and continued her walk down the quiet antiseptic hallway. She followed the yellow line past the desk and the restroom before turning the corner to her left. She looked up at the black placards mounted above each doorway.

"1022 . . . 1023 . . . 1024." Tina mumbled. She stopped just short of the doorway and listened in. She could hear the heart monitor beeping a steady, consistent rhythm, and two voices, talking softly. Tina didn't notice the nurse, carrying a vase of flowers coming out of Regina's room.

"May I help you?" asked the nurse sharply.

"I'm sorry. I was looking for. . ." Tina was cut off by Marcus.

"Tina! Good, you're here!" Marcus peered out the door from his seat beside his mother's bed. "It's alright, she's family," he said to the nurse.

Tina's eyes went immediately to Regina's bed. A fluffy comforter was draped over the hospital issued linens and there were dozens of flowers all over the room. Tina saw Regina sitting upright in full makeup with an elegant velvet bed jacket over her hospital gown.

"Regina, you look well . . . under the circumstances," was all Tina could muster. It was difficult seeing Regina like this. She wanted to remember Regina as a strong, powerful woman.

Regina smiled. "Thank you for coming, Tina. I can imagine this might be awkward for you."

Tina felt relieved. "Is it that obvious?"

Marcus smiled. "Mother and I asked you here for something very important. Please have a seat."

Tina sat, feeling very uneasy. "What is it? You know I'd do anything for you both."

"Yes. Tina. We know. After your presentation at the Summit House today, we wanted to respond to your proposal as quickly as possible," Regina said. "I hope you don't think it morbid, being invited to my deathbed to accept a design contract."

Tina waved off the comment. "Your deathbed. Ha. Regina. You look great. I have no doubt you'll be out of here in... wait. What?"

Marcus picked up a document from the bedside stand. He handed it to Tina.

"We are delighted to extend this contract to you as the exclusive designer and brand manager for the Summit House," said Marcus. Regina smiled.

Tina did a poor job of concealing her shock. "I wasn't expecting . . . a decision so . . . soon . . . I, uh. . ."

"Of course. Under the circumstances there really wasn't anyone else we could ask, was there?" Regina replied pointing to the watch now hanging around Tina's neck.

Tina stopped stammering and removed the watch from her neck. She looked at it -- stared at it, really -- as if for the first time.

"Will you accept our offer?" Marcus asked.

Tina thought back over the last few weeks, her chance encounter with this old lady and her son... and how everything in her life had been transformed in such a short period of time. She was lost in those thoughts when Regina's voice broke through the noise in her head.

"Tempus fugit, Dear One. It's not like I've got all week."

"What?" Tina snapped out of her trance. "Yes! Yes! Of course. I am honored to accept your offer." Regina smiled and relaxed back into the pillows.

"Then we just need your signature on the contract. We've both already signed. We'll have copies ready at the Summit House first thing in the morning," Marcus said.

"Certainly." Tina quickly scanned the document, signed it and handed it back to Marcus.

"Merry Christmas, Tina." Regina said. Before her young protegee and her son could get flustered she added, "Yes, I know Christmas was a few days ago. And a year or so ago I could have timed this whole thing a bit better." She sounded tired. "I'm old enough to declare that Christmas can be any time we gather with loved ones. Now if you'll both excuse me. Marcus, will you see Tina out?"

"Of course, Mother."

"Take some flowers with you. I'm not dead yet, and there'll be plenty more at the funeral, I'm sure," Regina said with a wink.

Tina and Marcus smiled at Regina. Marcus pulled a poinsettia off the nearby table and handed it to Tina. "Get some rest, Mother."

"Thank you, Son," Regina said. "And thank you, Tina."

Tina and Marcus walked along the yellow line back toward the nurse's station.

"It is a peculiar thing, isn't it?" Tina said, examining the watch in her hand.

"Indeed," Marcus said. "I suspect you've only got a few days left."

Tina nodded, knowing that she did not need to ask how she would recognize the final message. Instead she asked, "How long will it take me to find someone to pass it to?"

"You'll know when the time is right," Marcus replied.

Tina stopped short of the elevators and placed the poinsettia on the nurse's desk.

"Hold on," Tina said, "do you have a minute?" she asked with a bit of puzzlement in her voice. "I vaguely remember you saying something about Regina giving you this watch when you graduated from college."

"Yes, she passed it to me when I graduated."

"The day you met Milagra?" Tina asked.

"That very day." He smiled.

"Then why was she wearing it on the airplane the day I met her?"

"Remember when Mother told you about her estrangement from her father? When Milagra died, she and I experienced something similar," Marcus sighed. "She was traveling and couldn't make it back for the funeral because of some bad weather and missed connections. I was less than forgiving and felt all the 'family first' talk from the Secret Watch had been a lot of lip service. So I sent it back to her," he said.

"And she has had it ever since?"

"Yes. In retrospect, I was not thinking straight and acted from a place of pain and resentment. We reconciled in short order, but I never asked for the watch back. I didn't feel like I deserved it anymore. Besides, Mother continued to travel a lot and I forgot to ask about it when she was in town. On this trip home she said she was bringing it to me as sort of an 'extra' olive branch," Marcus smiled. "But when I saw Mother had given it to you, I knew you were the right person to have it."

"I still don't understand why either of you would give it to a total stranger," Tina shrugged.

"You know the drill, my friend: a few more days and you'll understand. Tick-tock," Marcus teased.

"Fair enough," Tina said. "Please keep me posted about your mother."

"I promise," Marcus replied. "I'm sure your family will be pleased with the news of the evening. Please travel safely. It has already started to snow."

"Thank you," Tina said as the elevator doors opened. She stepped inside and watched Marcus until the doors were completely closed. She pressed the button for the ground floor and began the trip back home.

18. The Best Gift

"Our deepest wounds surround our greatest gifts."
-- Ken Page

With all the chaos of Christmas under her belt, Tina felt a bit relieved to be going back to work -- this time as an official part of The Summit House organization. Her contract allowed her to keep her own identity as an entrepreneur, while allowing her to claim her rightful role in the redesign of a prestigious, well-known brand. In less than a day, as word spread about her new client, other businesses in the area began calling Tina to oversee their design projects.

Although it wasn't a surprise, Tina was still stunned when Marcus called from the hospital. Regina had died peacefully with her son by her side. The funeral was in two days and would be followed by a memorial gathering at The Manor. Tina pulled out her blue dress, white gloves and readied herself for the days ahead.

She glanced at the Secret Watch and read the day's inscription one more time:

"Life is short. Don't wait to enjoy it."

Somehow, the news of Regina's death didn't sadden Tina as much as she had expected. Instead, she felt a powerful wave of gratitude. Tina reflected briefly on the highs and lows of the day and the weeks leading up to it. Less than two months ago her business had been in shambles and she was full of fear about her family's future.

Tina cried both tears of sadness and gratitude: for Regina's influence, for the Secret Watch and for the new chapter in her life.

The next morning, Tina woke and hurriedly grabbed for the watch. For days she'd been waiting for the final inscription and wondered how she would know.

THE SECRET WATCH

Tina took out her notebook, opened the watch and read:

"The best gift you can give is attention. . .
and time."

Once the kids were off to school, Tina decided to put work aside for the day. "There's nothing that says I can't give a gift to myself when I need it . . . And right now I could really use a special gift."

She pulled out her old turntable, dusted off her vinyl records and spent hours with her favorite music. Tina danced around the living room, feeling more gratitude, vitality and joy than she had in years. She wasn't just dancing with her feet: her heart danced in celebration of her time with Regina.

When school let out, Tina read with Charlie and introduced Natalie to some of the music that she'd grown up on.

At first Natalie was confounded. "The discs are too big for our CD player, Mom." Mother and daughter shared a good laugh as Tina instructed Natalie in the use of the old turntable.

171

Everyone was in good spirits for the evening.

"Mom," Charlie asked. "Are you going to go see that lady who died?"

"Yes, Charlie," Tina replied. "Her name is Regina and I am going to visit her family tomorrow."

"Well, if she's dead, shouldn't you be sad?" he asked.

Tina took a deep breath and held Charlie tightly. "Part of me is very sad right now. She was a brand new and special friend. And her son Marcus just lost his mom. So yes, I'm sad. I'm also happy. I learned a lot from Regina. One of the best things she taught me is that life is short and we need to do our best to enjoy every bit of it."

Charlie seemed satisfied with the answer and skipped off to his room to play with his toys.

Tina savored the light-hearted moment all too aware that tomorrow would be a different story.

The next morning Tina woke gently. She lay in bed enjoying the morning sounds before reaching for her journal and the watch. Out of habit, she pressed the fob to open it. Nothing. She was not surprised.

"So *'The best gift you can give is attention . . . and time,'* was the last message for me," Tina said, thinking back to the night the Secret Watch had become part of her life.

She remembered how closed off she was. How annoyed she had been about some chatty old lady in a wheelchair. She remembered that Regina had seemed genuinely interested in her, even when she wanted to withdraw. She grew teary when she remembered the end of that flight: fast friends, sharing family stories, talking about everything from building a business to being a mother.

Tina sighed heavily, reflecting on the meaning of the final inscription and the way an apparently random act of kindness had created such enormous change in her life.

"She paid attention to what was going on beyond the few terse words I offered," Tina thought as she sat on the edge of her bed. She sobbed deeply, finally starting to mourn the loss of her new friend.

"I was so irritated with you," Tina said, looking skyward. "I didn't want to be bothered. I'm sorry. I am so sorry. I missed so much. Thank you for your time and persistent attention . . . Most of all, thank you for not letting me miss out on knowing you."

She began to regain her composure and heard her children in the hall. They were readying themselves for the funeral and, of course, arguing while they did. Fortunately for Tina, Michael was in 'time and attention mode,' ready on the scene to redirect the kids and keep them on task.

Tina rose from her bedside, applied makeup and finished dressing. She donned her white gloves and hat and walked into the hallway.

19. Without Expectation

"There is no exercise better for the heart than reaching down and lifting people up." -- John A. Holmes, Jr.

The service was beautiful. So many notable characters from Regina's long life came to pay their respects. The choir sang sweet hymns of praise and thanksgiving.

Marcus and his children were seated up front. He insisted that Tina and her family sit near them. She accepted and kept an ear keenly tuned for the slightest hint of trouble from her two children. To their credit, both Natalie and Charlie demonstrated exemplary behavior throughout the church service. Michael praised them as they returned to the car.

As Michael pulled into the drive of The Manor, both Natalie and Charlie gasped and stared in wonder at the enormous home. Tina smiled at them, remembering how she felt when she pulled into that driveway for the first time.

Robert directed guests from the parking area to the house. He tipped his hat to Tina, who responded with a hug and her condolences.

"You obviously cared very deeply for Mrs. King, Robert," Tina said.

"Yes, ma'am. She was a rare gem. We'll all miss her," Robert replied, trying to hide his tears.

Tina brought her family around to the door of the summer kitchen; she wanted the house to unfold for them in much the same way it had on her first visit. When they reached the foyer, they met George, taking coats and offering condolences.

"Thank you, George," Tina said.

"It's the least I could do for you, Mrs. Williams," George replied. "And this is your family?"

"Yes, George. My husband, Michael, daughter Natalie and my son, Charlie."

"Pleased to meet you all," said George. "Charlie, I believe you'll find some entertaining activities in the study. Natalie, there's a whole library of music in the living room. Your mother told me you play the piano."

"Yes, I do," Natalie responded happily. "Mom said there's an old piano in there."

"Actually, it's called a melodion, Natalie," George corrected. "Allow me to introduce you."

Natalie looked hopeful and Tina smiled, thanking George for making her family feel so welcome.

"Not at all, Mrs. Williams," George replied. "I'm happy to help."

Marcus caught Tina's eye. She smiled as he crossed to her.

"I'm so sorry about Regina," Tina began. She turned slightly to bring Michael into the conversation. "This is my husband Michael," she said.

"I wish we were meeting under better circumstances, Marcus," Michael said. "From everything Tina has told me your mother was quite a remarkable woman."

"Yes. Thank you," Marcus said, somewhat distracted. Someone or something had caught his eye.

"Marcus? Is everything OK?" Tina asked. "I mean aside from the obvious? You seem a bit distracted."

"Yes, Tina. Sorry. I'm concerned about George," he said.

Michael excused himself and went to check on Charlie. Tina saw the worried look on Marcus' face and turned to search for George. She spotted him coming out of the living room. He certainly didn't appear to be stressed. To Tina he looked just like George: competent and compassionate. Attending to the comfort of others. Quietly in charge.

Tina turned back to Marcus. It was *his* reaction that concerned her.

"What do you mean? He has been the most remarkable help today," Tina said. "I don't think I've ever seen him work so hard. And George Entrega has never been a slacker."

"That's just it, Tina," Marcus replied, riveted by George's coming and going around the room. "George has always been a hard worker. He has been our most loyal employee . . . since I was a teen. I didn't hire him to tend to things today, though. I've got temps for that. I invited him as a guest: he is as much a part of the family as some of my relatives. Still, he insisted on helping. Said it was the least he could do for us."

Tina could certainly appreciate George's desire to give back to the King family. She remembered the times she talked to George while preparing for her presentation; he'd shared several ways that working for the Kings had enriched his life. George was grateful and deeply devoted to the family. She also suspected that there was no point in trying to explain it to Marcus right now.

She stood silently beside Marcus for a couple of minutes, watching George from across the foyer. He was collecting coats, greeting guests, directing traffic and connecting people with others already in the house.

"Do you suppose he thinks he is going to lose his job?" she asked.

Marcus sighed. "I certainly hope not. No one knows more about The Summit House than George. As you said in your presentation the other day, he's the glue that holds it all together."

"I remember," said Tina. "Maybe this is how he processes grief," she suggested. "Have you talked with him?"

"I tried," Marcus replied. "Before you arrived, I spent a few minutes alone with George. I reminded him that he was as much a guest here today as anyone else. I took the opportunity to express my appreciation for his support -- to remind him of how much he's needed at The Summit House and, frankly, in my life. Now more than ever. . ." he trailed off.

"What did he say?" Tina asked softly.

Marcus laughed a little. "Naturally, he insisted he was fine. In fact I believe his exact words were: 'I promised your parents I would always do my best to serve the King family. Today is no different. There is plenty of time for my grief.'"

Thinking back about her brief encounters with George, Tina was struck by something a little odd. George seemed taller each time they met. She smiled to herself, recalling the nervousness that threatened to overwhelm her first few visits to The

Summit House. It could have easily kept her from connecting with George . . . much as her fear and bitterness had almost kept her from letting Regina into her life.

She remembered George's keen insights about the inscription: *'Good enough rarely is. Not enough always is.'* His explanation that day had been a big help.

Then, remembering her very last inscription, a smile played across Tina's face. She grabbed Marcus by the arm and laughed out loud.

"What are you laughing about?" Marcus asked. "I am really quite worried about George. I don't think that is even a little bit funny. . ."

Emboldened by inspiration Tina cut him off. With one hand on each of his shoulders to ensure proper eye contact she slowly said, "Sometimes, the best gift you can give is attention . . . and time."

A knowing look came over Marcus' face. His tension eased. "The final inscription?"

Tina nodded. Her new co-conspirator smiled, relieved and grateful at what he knew would come next.

"Brilliant! Perfectly brilliant, Mrs. Williams,"
Marcus said, hugging her to his side as his face
crinkled in delight.

Tina recognized the look on his face from the first
night they'd met -- the night Regina gave her the
mysterious Secret Watch.

"George!" Marcus boomed across the noisy room.

"Yes, Mr. King? Is there something you need?"
George was eager, but not anxious.

"Actually, George, there is. Tina, would you do the
honors?" he asked playfully. Tina and Marcus smiled
in much the same way Marcus had smiled with his
mother a few weeks earlier.

Tina put her hand over her heart for a moment
before closing it around the beautiful little watch
hanging from a chain around her neck. She
breathed deeply and removed it with one hand.
With the other she reached out to George.

Pressing the antique watch securely into George's
hand Tina said, "This is for you, with appreciation
and gratitude for all your attention and care."

George opened his hand to examine the watch. His face was suddenly serious, then wide-eyed.

"This is Mr. King's . . . I mean Mrs. King's . . . I mean . . . Mrs. Williams, this is your watch!"

"No, George," Tina corrected. "Now it belongs to you. I'm confident it will help you on your journey."

"Be sure to read the inscription," said Marcus quietly. "It just might surprise you."

George clasped the watch between his hands, closed his eyes for a moment and whispered a very quiet "Thank you so much." Then, straightening a bit, he looked around the room and noticed some confusion near the kitchen.

"With your kind permission. . ."

"Of course, George. You know where to find us," said Marcus with a grin.

Tina and Marcus stood side by side, watching the now-slightly-taller George provide leadership and comfort to the frazzled temps.

Marcus looked toward his new friend and said, "Here we go. I assume you're free for lunch at The Summit House this week?"

Tina smiled widely. "I'll be there with bells on."

Acknowledgments

When I was a kid, I used to imagine the day I'd win an Oscar and, for a joke, I'd walk on stage with a scroll under my arm, unfurl it, and begin reading the names of all the people I wanted to thank. It never dawned on me that I might actually craft such a list.

First, and foremost to God, for inspiring this story and putting these wonderful people in my life. I count these folks as blessings and I'm grateful. Second, to Andrea Patten for her tireless editing of my bad punctuation -- not to mention a couple of frantic 'voice changes.' Such a process probably would have killed any other friendship; instead, this one got stronger. You are "THE woman" when it comes to finding the purest meaning behind my words. Your faith in this project kept me from saying "good enough" when we both know "good enough rarely is." You are truly a gem.

To Liz, who actually tried to dissuade me from writing this book: you forced me to tighten things up and make the story even stronger. Larry Bienemann: your candid disdain for "his polished shoes" gave me an opportunity to stick to my guns; your professional opinion gave me hope the book was decent. Thanks for both.

Bob Burg, Amy Oscar, Josh Alward, Rhiannon Llewellyn, Chris Harney, Nancy Korzyniewski, and all the early readers of this book: many thanks. To read a work in progress is a lot to ask of anyone. You were most generous and gracious with your time and your input. I hope you like the way it was used. And Lisa Wilber for the same . . . except in typical Lisa fashion you went "above and beyond" . . . submitting your input from a vacation overseas!

Lori "Flirty Grrl" Paquette: you not only designed a gorgeous cover, you inspired two of the characters. I miss you every time I can't see you. Esteri Hinman and your proof-reading eagle eye: thank you for finding things we stopped seeing several drafts ago.

Stevie, wherever you are, thanks for finding me on that airplane and channeling the title and idea for this book. You were right about the title and the story. Here's hoping the 'bestseller' part is true as well.

To my coach and friend, Teresa Romain: your faith in my words, my work, and my talent allowed me to "remove the red glasses" more often. Your continued friendship and support allow me to experience abundance more frequently, and to practice "having" and "receiving". I didn't know I had it in me, and it's wonderful. Thank you.

To my CIP peeps: Lori F., Sarah, Judi, Ted, Erin, Tami and Dana, you saw me through all the #fuh, and I can't thank you enough. To my Soul Caller tribe: you give me so much space to be me and I'm humbled by your stories of light and life. To the BW/EE folks who volunteered to review cover designs, read early drafts, and generally keep me from losing faith in this project: I heart you very much. Women of The Realm -- especially Rhonda -- there aren't enough words to express the value you add to my life. To my Vertigo family: Ted, Jacque, Jen, Matt, Steve, Dave, Kasie, Dan, Heather, Gary "Monstro" King, and the rest I give you my undying gratitude for being so creative, so awesome and holding me accountable to excellence.

To my family and closest friends, some of whom I've already mentioned, you've made so much of my life what it is today. I do not forget where I come from. Thank you to The Aunts for being my surrogate mom from time to time.

Extra special thanks to Mike Bradley for the tour of The Manor House, taking care of "the cupcake" and for being a generally excellent human being. Your open-heartedness led me to Marcus and Regina. Thank you.

To Martin Jennings, my high school drama teacher, for telling me to share what I know. You meant it in a different way, but I've always been a bit contrary.

Finally, "my boys." Thank you Ben, Forest and Liam for helping me "work when it's time to work" and "play when it's time to play." We might not always get it right but you always make me want to. I love you.

About The Author

 Lisa Robbin Young was a storyteller at an early age. An award-winning writer before she graduated middle school, Lisa is also an accomplished performer and musician. She is currently working on her third full-length album: a collection of inspirational jazz, soul & pop tunes.

Lisa's also faced the ups and downs of being an entrepreneur for nearly 20 years. Since building one of the first-ever e-commerce websites in the early 1990's, Lisa's business experience spans a diverse array of creative industries. She's also a coach to authors, artists, and creative entrepreneurs, helping them to build a noble empire and live an inspired life. Her latest venture, an entertainment media company, is in development.

LisaRobbinYoung.com

The Inscriptions

There are 60 inscriptions from The Secret Watch.
Receive a complimentary copy of all the inspiring
inscriptions when you register on our website:

TheSecretWatch.com

Advance Praise for *The Secret Watch*

"I absolutely recommend you read *The Secret Watch* as soon as you can. You will be gripped, dying to see what happens next. Once I started reading it I couldn't put it down and had to finish it in one sitting - very rare for me nowadays!"
      - Carol Dodsley, www.how2getsocial.com

"I plan on writing all the inscriptions on a piece of paper and picking one out everyday!"
      –   **Laurie LaFalce,** Division Manager, *Park Lane Jewelry*

–

"The Secret Watch teaches not only lessons of life, love and business, but it also has certain metaphysical qualities that are just subtle enough and obvious enough to catch the older philosopher's attention."
      - Josh Alward, student

"I loved the story line. I laughed, I cried and wrote all the inscriptions in my journal. I would recommend this book to career individuals, to young adults who have just completed college and about to start their careers entrepreneurs, especially if they are already parents."

- **Shana Barnett**, online marketing consultant & web devloper, www.shanakaybarnett.com

"The Secret Watch tells a story that is bigger than what it looks like at first glance. An enjoyable read with lots of inspiration!"

- **Tea Silvestre**, Small Business Marketing Coach, www.thewordchef.com

"The book was delightful. I was actually sorry to have it end."

- *John Skowronek, OSHA Trainer & Consultant, Square One Solutions, www.worksq1.com*

"The Secret Watch is a delightful story about living with intention. The lessons are timeless and simple.... be hopeful, trust that you are where you are meant to be, be open to the possibilities and the people who have been placed in your path. Nothing is by accident. The entrepreneur heroine grasps the potential of her life and passes the baton with gratitude."

- **Nancy Korzyniewski**, Direct selling coach and trainer, former field services manager, www.nancycoaches.com

"*The Secret Watch* is a wonderfully compelling story that leaves the reader wanting to develop the types of relationships that Lisa's characters have. The messages revealed throughout the story, and the way they impact and instruct the main character, left me looking at ways to weave these same lessons into my own life."
-**Rick Brown**, Founder, Rick Brown Communications, AvoidAMediaMeltdown.com

"Once I started reading *The Secret Watch* I couldn't stop: it was moving and wonderful . . . and like reading about a part of myself. I loved the lessons, beautifully wrapped in the story of the watch and a woman's desire to become 'more' -- for herself and for her family."
- **Melissa H. Dery**, Administrative Consultant, Owner, www.TheGoldenRuleVA.com

"The Secret Watch is a parable especially for entrepreneurs and solo-preneurs; If you're one, you'll easily recognize the "Tina" in you. And like Tina, you should take the timeless messages of the watch to heart and use them to get out of your stuck places. When you do, you'll discover a whole new world of opportunities."
- **Annie Bartlett**, solo-preneur

"A beautiful story about the greatness in each of us. And how embracing -- and growing -- that greatness can lead to riches more valuable than gold!"

> **- Chris Harney**, Rendi National Field Developer & *direct sales coach,*
> *www.chrisharney.com*

"Lisa Robbin Young's book "The Secret Watch" is written from a rare place of love, compassion, empathy & hard-eyed business sense. Lisa knows how to tell a story, she creates believable characters and each chapter contains bits of business and personal wisdom that are instantly usable.

The best kinds of wisdom are those that, upon reading, you say to yourself, "Hmm, that's so simple. I should have known that." Lisa's book is filled with those "Hmmm" moments.

Read this book. Incorporate two pieces of wisdom per week into your life from The Secret Watch. And then, just watch what happens."

> **- David Stanley**, teacher, athlete, cancer survivor, dstan58.blogspot.com

Made in the USA
Charleston, SC
13 December 2013